Report on China's FinTech FIRE Index

(2021)

Chief Editor　HU Bin
Associate Editors　YIN Zhentao　WANG Yong

Abstract: FinTech (Financial Technology) is a financial innovation driven by technology. The new generation of information technology represented by big data, artificial intelligence, cloud computing, and blockchain has fully penetrated into many financial subdivisions, and is changing and reshaping the financial industry. The sound development of FinTech is conducive to improving the quality and efficiency of financial services, and has become an important support to the financial competitiveness of many countries.

The *Report on China's FinTech FIRE Index in* 2021 consists of Chinese and English chapters. Among them, the English chapters are translated version of the Chinese ones. The Chinese version mainly contains six chapters. The first chapter is an overview of FinTech, which defines the concept of FinTech, summarizes the basic characteristics of FinTech, and reviews the top ten events of China's FinTech in 2020. The second chapter is the introduction of the index and its principle of construction. It introduces China's FinTech FIRE Index and explains the main data sources of the report. The third chapter is the main part of China's FinTech FIRE Index. It evaluates the overall development of FinTech in 59 large and medium-sized cities in China, and divides them into five classes based on the scores of each city, and investigates them from the perspectives of Factor, Intelligence, Resources and Enterprises. The fourth chapter is case analysis, a multi-angle and multi-dimensional comparative analysis of the development and progress of FinTech in the selected cities of the four classes is done in this chapter. The fifth chapter is the regional distribution of FinTech and its position in the industrial chain. With the chain of "bottom technology research and development—

technology integration output—financial scenario construction", the positions of FinTech enterprises in the FinTech industrial chain are designated, and the distribution characteristics of FinTech in perspectives of region, industrial chain and technology are explored. The sixth chapter is conclusions and prospects. Based on the main conclusions of the report, it puts forward specific policy recommendations for the development of FinTech in China, and prospects the development of FinTech in China.

Key Words: FinTech; Index; Digital Technology; Regulatory Technology

Preface

FinTech is a financial innovation driven by technology. With the continuous application of emerging technologies, such as mobile Internet, artificial intelligence, big data, cloud computing and blockchain, in maturity transformation, credit conversion, revenue conversion and risk conversion, FinTech not only upgrades and innovates the concept, way of thinking, processes and business mode of financial services, but also strengthens the integration function of resources and elements of the financial system. FinTech has become an important support for the financial competitiveness of many countries, and also represents the future trend of the development of the financial industry.

FinTech is characterized by "disruptive" innovations of trans-industry, disintermediation, decentralization and self-service, which pose major challenges to the financial regulation system, challenging the balance between financial innovation and financial regulation. Compared with the traditional financial sector, FinTech innovations are more virtual, convenient and sophisticated, leaving it more difficult to identify and verify financial risks. Moreover, risks are accumulated and transmitted more corectly, confronting regulators with greater challenges. They are urgently needed to upgrade and improve the regulation mechanism, to make sure that FinTech innovations are advanced safely and smoothly under prudent regulation, to help FinTech better serve the real economy, and to foster a new development paradigm with dual circulations.

In August 2019, the People's Bank of China issued the *Financial Technology (FinTech) Development Plan (2019 – 2021)*, which calls for adhering to the basic principles of "keeping to the right path and making innovations, ensuring safe and controllable creations, providing the most accessible welfare for the people, and upholding open and win-win spirit", and giving full play to FinTech to promote the high-quality development of China's financial industry. As is stated in the *Proposal of the CPC Central Committee on Formulating the Fourteenth Five-Year Plan for National Economic and Social Development and the Vision for the Year 2035* adopted in November 2020, financial technology should be promoted to enhance financial inclusion. So, how to guide the healthy and sustainable development of the FinTech industry, ensure that financial innovation is carried out under the prudent supervision, and promote FinTech to better serve the real economy, have become important issues for the construction of the modern financial system.

The rapid development of FinTech in China has expanded the availability and coverage of financial services, and narrowed their spatial heterogeneity, leading the global FinTech wave in many aspects. At present, FinTech in China has gone into the "deep water zone", where high-speed development is transforming to high-quality development, during which, problems and risks accumulated in the earlier period are gradually exposed and regulatory measures for FinTech are correspondingly strengthened. In this context, how to objectively measure the overall level of China's fintech development and its global status, assess the discrepancy in FinTech development between different regions, and figure out the regional and industrial chain distribution characteristics of FinTech enterprises, have become hot issues to common concern to the local governments, regulatory authorities and the industry.

To this end, young research fellows from the department of FinTech of the Institute of Finance and Banking under the Chinese Academy of Social Sciences, have conducted collective research based on data from 59 major cities in China, to work out the China's FinTech FIRE Index, a FinTech evaluation index system, consisting of 4 first-level indicators, 9 second-level indicators and 21 third-level indicators, from four aspects of Factors, Intelligence, Resources and Enterprises. *The Report on China's FinTech FIRE Index (2021)* was also written to promote further research on FinTech, and to help the industry, regulators and local governments better understand the development of FinTech, identify its bottlenecks and obstacles, determine the direction of the growing FinTech, deal with its vulnerable spots, and promote the healthy and sustainable development of FinTech.

President Xi Jinping has stressed that to achieve high-quality development, we mustachieve innovation-driven connotative growth. We need to vigorously enhance our capacity for independent innovation and realize key and core technologies as soon as possible. This is an issue of vital importance to China's overall development, and it is also the key to forming a domestic cycle as the main body. As a top national think-tank, the Institute of Finance and Banking under the Chinese Academy of Social Sciences sincerely hope that, with the China's FinTech FIRE Index as a starting point, researches on FinTech should be done more intensively and extensively, to make recommendations to the CPC Central Committee and the State Council, provide research support for the local financial development, promote the healthy and sustainable development of the FinTech industry, so to increase global competitiveness of China's financial industry.

August, 2021

Key points of the report

1. China's FinTech FIRE Index Ranking

First, according to the ranking, Beijing, Shanghai and Shenzhen are ranked the top three, followed by Hangzhou, Guangzhou, Nanjing, Wuhan, Chengdu, Suzhou and Xi'an, from 4 to 10. In terms of spatial distribution, developed regions in the southeast have obvious advantages in the development of FinTech, and some cities in the central and western regions also have good performance.

Second, from the perspective of Factors, Beijing tops the chart, apparently superior in both economy and population. Hangzhou ranks the second with its advantages in demographic dividend, especially in population growth. Guangzhou, Shanghai, Chongqing, Chengdu, Shenzhen, Changsha, Wuhan and Xi'an are the rest of the top 10 in order.

Third, in terms of Intelligence, Beijing outperforms the others for its absolute strength in research both in enterprises and universities. The next two are Shanghai and Nanjing, which are comparatively advantageous in research. Guangzhou, Shenzhen,

Hangzhou, Wuhan, Chengdu, Xi'an and Tianjin rank 4 to 10.

Fourth, from the perspective of Resources, Shanghai takes the first place with its advantages in policy resources, Internet resources and financial resources. Beijing and Shenzhen ranked the second and third, respectively, due to their outstanding performance in Internet resources and financial resources. Wuhan, Hangzhou, Nanjing, Chengdu, Guiyang, Xi'an and Guangzhou are the following 4 to 10.

Fifth, as for Enterprises, Beijing is in the lead, in both the quantity and quality of enterprises. Shenzhen, Shanghai, Hangzhou, Guangzhou, Suzhou, Nanjing, Wuhan, Chengdu and Jinan take the places from 2 to 10.

2. The Regional and Industrial Chain Distribution of FinTech Enterprises

First, in terms of the number of FinTech enterprises, Beijing, Shanghai, Shenzhen, Guangzhou, Hangzhou, Chengdu, Nanjing, Suzhou, Wuhan and Tianjin are the top 10 in order. Among them, FinTech enterprises in Beijing, Shanghai and Shenzhen respectively account for 19.5%, 13.0% and 12.3% of the total. The majority of FinTech enterprises are situated in the middle of the industry chain (74.2%), followed by that in the upstream (21.4%), and then that in the downstream (4.4%).

Second, when it comes to patent applications, Beijing, Shenzhen, Shanghai, Guangzhou, Hangzhou, Suzhou, Chengdu, Nanjing, Jinan and Zhengzhou rank the top 10 in the chart. The number of patents in the middle of the industrial chain is the largest, taking up 85.1% of the whole, followed by those in the upstream of the industrial chain (12.9%), and the fewest goes to the downstream of the industrial chain, only 2.0%.

Third, in the field of digital technology, companies engaged in big data research and development are the most, followed by those in cloud computing, blockchain and artificial intelligence. As for the number of patents, that of big data is the largest, those of cloud computing and artificial intelligence are the second and third largest, while that of blockchain is the smallest. However, in terms of the average quality of patents, blockchain ranks the highest, followed by cloud computing, artificial intelligence, while big data ranks the lowest.

3. Policy Recommendations

First, to strengthen policy support and promote the development of financial technology. The government should introduce a development plan for the FinTech industry, and provide more supports for its development. With the help of policy support, the allocation of funds should be guided rationally, more investment in FinTech enterprises, especially small and medium-sized ones, so as to solve the financing difficulties encountered by small and medium-sized enterprises.

Second, to find the right entry point for the development of FinTech based on local conditions. For Beijing, Shanghai and Shenzhen, where FinTech is well developed, they should sustain a virtuous circle of innovation stimulating research and development to promote technology, and technology in turn enabling scenarios. Other cities should develop FinTech in accordance with their comparative advantages to search for breakthroughs.

Third, to accelerate the construction of financial infrastructure, taking the introduction of digital currency by the central bank as an opportunity. Digital RMB was piloted in 2020, and the digital currencies are to change the financial infrastructure profoundly. At present, the People's Bank of China has basically established the system framework of "two databases and three centers" for digital currency issuance and digital wallets for consumers. Local governments should take this opportunity to amplify the construction of key financial infrastructure and promote the application of emerging technologies, such as blockchain, big data, cloud computing and digital wallets, in digital currencies.

Fourth, city clusters should be established in the northern region to promote the locally coordinated development of financial technology. Experience of the southern region should be used for reference, while developing FinTech in the north, where city clusters, like the Beijing-Tianjin-Hebei cluster, should be set up to strengthen regional cooperation, to maintain regional integrity, to devote greater policy efforts to advance regional economic integration, to enhance regional interactions between cities, and to realize the coordinated development of financial technology.

Fifth, cities in the central and western regions should take the opportunity of developing financial technology to achieve all-round development. In recent years, emerging technologies, such as big data, artificial intelligence andblockchain, have been widely applied in the financial sector, making the integration of finance and technology go deeper and deeper. The central and western regions should follow this trend to encourage theoretical research on FinTech, deepen the cooperation between industry, education and research, and accelerate the transformation of research results to real products and services. Moreover, FinTech should be actively used to provide better financial services for countries on the "Belt and Road" Initiatine, to achieve comprehensive development in these regions.

Sixth, to strengthen the construction of regulation technology and improve the effectiveness of local financial regulation. According to the local financial regulation requirements of industrial supervision, risk monitoring and warning, coordinated regulation and FinTech service management, regulation technology should be reinforced in practice, such as off-sight supervision over traditional services and regulatory sandboxes for innovative businesses, both of which should be assisted with on-sight regulation. Only in this way, can the capacity and efficiency of local financial regulation be improved.

Contents

1 An Overview of FinTech ······ (1)
   1.1 The Definition ······ (1)
   1.2 The Characteristics ······ (2)
   1.3 Ten FinTech Events in 2020 ······ (6)

2 Introduction to the FinTech FIRE Index ······ (15)
   2.1 The FinTech FIRE Index ······ (15)
   2.2 Data Sources ······ (18)

3 China's FinTech FIRE Index ······ (20)
   3.1 The Index ······ (20)
   3.2 The Four Sub-indexes ······ (25)

4 Case Studies ······ (39)
   4.1 The First Class: Beijing, Shanghai and Shenzhen ······ (39)
   4.2 The Second Class: Hangzhou, Guangzhou and Chengdu ······ (44)

4.3 The Third Class: Suzhou and Zhengzhou .... (49)
 4.4 The Fourth Class: Guiyang and Foshan .... (52)
 4.5 The Fifth Class .... (55)

5 **Distribution Characteristics of FinTech in Cities and Industrial Chains** .... (57)
 5.1 The Distribution of FinTech Enterprises .... (59)
 5.2 The Distribution of FinTech Patents .... (62)
 5.3 The Distribution of Digital Technology of FinTech .... (65)

6 **Conclusions and Prospects** .... (69)
 6.1 Conclusions .... (69)
 6.2 Policy Recommendations .... (72)
 6.3 Prospects .... (75)

Postscript .... (79)

1
An Overview of FinTech

1.1 The Definition

FinTech, or Financial Technology, is a blending word of Financial and Technology. The Financial Stability Board (FSB) defined the concept of FinTech in its report *Financial Stability Implications from FinTech, Supervisory and Regulatory Issues that Merit Authorities Attention* released in 2017, saying that "FinTech is technology-enabled innovation in financial services, particularly driven by emerging technologies, such as big data, blockchain, cloud computing and artificial intelligence, which could result in new business models, applications, processes or products with an associated significant effect on financial markets and the provision of financial services". The Basel Committee on Banking Supervision (BCBS) identifies FinTech with four categories according to its survey conducted in 2017, which are the Payments, Clearing & Settlement category, the Deposits, Lending & Capital Raising category, the Investment Management category, and the Market

Provisioning category. According to the People's Bank of China, FinTech refers to technology-driven financial innovation, whose essence is that licensed financial institutions upgrade or innovate financial products, business models and processes with modern technological achievements in compliance with the law and regulations, so as to improve the quality and efficiency of financial development (People's Bank of China, 2019).

From the supply side, it can be defined as broadly as "FinTech" and narrowly as "FinTech". In a broad sense, FinTech participants involve both technology companies and traditional financial institutions, as long as they conduct finance services with technology. While in a narrow sense, FinTech specifically refers to those small, technologically advanced new entrants to financial services (not including large technology companies entering financial services) or financial institutions that focuses on technology. This report uses the broad term "FinTech", believing that FinTech covers financial businesses of start-ups as well as large technology companies, and the technological application of traditional financial institutions.

1.2 The Characteristics

1.2.1 Innovative

The essence of FinTech is to apply evolving technology in the financial sector to drive financial innovation and generate new business models, applications, processes or products, to improve the efficiency and reduce the costs of financial services with a safe, controllable, advanced and efficient FinTech application system. With a new round of scientific and technological revolution, emerging technologies, such as big data (Box 1), artificial intelligence (Box 2), cloud computing (Box 3) and blockchain (Box 4), are closely integrated with financial businesses, making contributions to the development of FinTech.

Box 1

Big data is a big set of high-speed, complex and variable data, which requires advanced technologies to complete its collection, storage, distribution, management and analysis. IBM and Oracle summarized its characteristics from the 5V perspectives, which are Volume, Velocity, Variety, Value density and Veracity.

Source: Chebbi et al. (2015), https://link.springer.com/chapter/10.1007/978-3-319-24306-1_62#citeas

---

Box 2

The term artificial intelligence was raised in 1955 by John McCarthy, emeritus professor at Stanford University, to refer to "the sciences and technologies that produce intelligent devices". Much of the research involves programming machines to act intelligently, for example, playing chess. But nowadays we put more emphasis on machines being able to learn like humans.

Source of data: Artificial Intelligence Definitions, Stanford University.

Box 3

Cloud computing is a network accessible mode, through which elastic and shared physical and virtual resources pools are provided and managed on demand. Cloud computing consists of key characteristics, cloud computing roles and activities, cloud capabilities and cloud services, cloud deployment models, and cloud computing focuses.

Source of data: Information Technology-Cloud Computing-Overview and Vocabulary.

Box 4

Blockchains are immutable distributed digital ledgers that are protected with advanced encryption techniques, replicating between peer-to-peer nodes in a peer-to-peer network, and agree on transaction logs by using a consensus mechanism, where control is dispersed. In a typical blockchain system, data are generated and stored in blocks, which are chronologically linked into a chain like data structure.

Source of data: Gamage et al. (2012), https://link..springer.com/article/10.1007/s42979-020-00123-0#citeas

1.2.2 Inclusive

FinTech is inclusive. On the one hand, integrated with finance and technology, FinTech expands the scope, lowers the costs and threshold, and improves the quality of financial services, so that a wider range of people, especially long-tail[①] customers, can enjoy better and more efficient financial services. On the other hand, the rapid development of FinTech has resulted in many new financial business models, processes, products and services, which provide small and medium enterprises with not only financial supports but also ideas and solutions to overcome the difficulties of expensive financing.

1.2.3 Integrated

FinTech is integrated, for the application of emerging digital technologies to the financial sector has achieved the integration of finance and technology, financial sector and other commercial sectors, financial institutions and technology companies. First, financial institutions use FinTech to promote digital transformation and the integration of finance and technology. Second, the cross-sector cooperation between traditional financial institutions and technology companies is going further, giving full play to their respective strengths, and constantly upgrading financial services and products. Third, the integration of finance and technology can incubate evolving business forms of FinTech, such as online payments, digital currencies, and intelligent investment.[②]

[①] Long-tail customers are derived from the long-tail theory proposed by Chris Anderson, editor-in-chief of the American "Wired" magazine in 2004, which refers to customers whose demand for products or services is small and scattered, and the long tail of the demand curve is constructed.

[②] A robo-advisor can be defined as "a self-guided online wealth management service that provides automated investment advice at low costs and low account minimums, employing portfolio management algorithms".

1.2.4 Instructive

The development of FinTech is instructive to the upgrading of the financial sector. First, it is instructive to financial innovation. Emerging technologies are playing an increasingly prominent role in the development of finance, which not only brings the innovation of financial products, services, models and processes, but also contributed to the update of financial activities. Second, it is instructive to the evolution of technology. The continuous innovation of FinTech enables technology companies to upgrade the financial industry with their technological advantages, and also leads the digitalization of traditional financial institutions and reshapes their services and platforms. Third, the progress of FinTech drives the reform of financial regulation. The development of FinTech leaves a profound impact on financial regulation. In order to prevent new challenges and risks caused by FinTech and meet the regulatory requirements, reforms of financial regulation should be promoted and improved regulatory system of FinTech should be established.

1.3 Ten FinTech Events in 2020

In 2020, the COVID-19 pandemic wreaked havoc around the world. This report selects 10 major events in FinTech to map the development of FinTech in China of the year.

1.3.1 Stopping Peer-to-Peer (P2P) Online Lenders

The number of P2P online lenders in operation in China

gradually decreased from 5,000 to 0 by the middle of November 2020. Those P 2P lenders were operated under strict supervision since 2016, and finally got eliminated by 2020.

Comments: The elimination of online lenders is resulted from many factors, including the concentrated outbreak of online lending risks, the mass exposure of online lending problems, the strict liquidation from the regulators and the macroeconomic downturn brought by the pandemic. However, elimination of these online lenders does not mean the end of the event. We should pay attention to the resolution of existing risks. Multiple measures should be taken to collect the escaped and bad debts, in order to recover funds to maintain financial stability and prevent risk expanding. At the same time, we should carefully draw lessons from the rectification of P2P online lenders, enhance supervision and regularize the development of the industry. Financial innovation can never go beyond supervision.

1.3.2 The Rapid Development of Contactless Finance

The sudden outbreak of the pandemic and the surging demand for "contactless services" have given rise to the development of new FinTech-based business models such as online, intelligent and digital "contactless" finance, which becomes an important weapon for financial institutions to cope with the impact of the pandemic and resume business growth.

Comments: The China Banking and Insurance Regulatory Commission issued the *Notice on Further Improving Financial Services for Epidemic Prevention and Control* in February 2020, requiring all banking and insurance institutions to promote online business, optimize and multiply the channels of "contactless services", and provide safe and convenient "home" financial services. In this case, "contactless finance" develops with the pandemic. FinTech fully demonstrates the value of enabled finance and has made difference to the strategic layout, business scope and cooperation mode of financial institutions.

1.3.3 Record High Fines on Payments

In 2020, regulators kept exercising strict supervision over the third-party payment violations. The People's Bank of China issued more than 60 fines to payment institutions in 2020, with fines totaling more than 300-million-yuan, double that of the year before, according to an incomplete statistic report by reporters with the "Beijing Business Today" on Dec Cember 17.

Comments: In 2020, the regulatory authorities enhanced the rectification of the wrong doings in the payment industry, as well as intensified the supervision over this industry, with anti-money laundering and the provisions the key areas of supervision. The number of fines and the total amount of penalties hit a new high, and the number of large-amount fines obviously increased. The regulators imposed heavy penalties on those who had repeatedly violated the regulations and rules. The highest even reached 116 millionyuan. In addition, regulators enforced "double penalties" on payment institutions, involving nearly half of the fines. The supervision from the central bank were more targeted, with relevant institutions and responsible person severely penalized.

1.3.4 More Regulatory Sandboxes

The People's Bank of China launched a pilot program of "regulatory sandbox"[①] on FinTech in Beijing in December 2019. By now, the pilot supervision over FinTech innovation has been expanded from Beijing to Shanghai, Chongqing, Shenzhen, Xiong'an New Area, Hangzhou, Suzhou, Guangzhou and Chengdu, all of which have released lists of FinTech applications under pilot supervision.

Comments: With continuous expansion of pilot supervision over FinTech innovations, many licensed financial institutions and technology companies are exploring the use of emerging technologies to promote financial innovations, to accelerate digital transformation of traditional finance, and to facilitate finance better serve the real economy, while meeting compliance and risk manageable obligations. When risks are generally controllable, the regulators use the regulatory sandbox as a long-term effective way trying to establish a FinTech regulatory system customized to China, which can not only prevent financial risks, but also agree with rational innovations, in order, to realize transformations from passive regulation to proactive regulation, from static regulation to dynamic regulation, and from regulating with rules to with principles.

[①] A regulatory sandbox is a 'safe space' in which businesses can test innovative products, services, business models and delivery mechanisms without immediately incurring all the normal regulatory consequences of engaging in the activity in question.

1.3.5 More Pilot Cities for Digital RMB

In 2020, the digital RMB was piloted in cities across the country, and will continue to access more cities. Now it is being tested in Shenzhen, Suzhou, Xiong'an, Chengdu and scenarios of the approaching Winter Olympic Games. New pilot cities will further be added on the list and more application scenarios are to be tested.

Comments: The digital RMB is under test in a growing number of cities and its application scenarios are being diversified, from shopping to wage payment, transportation, traveling and other payments, which are accepted by more and more consumers. The issuance of digital RMB by the People's Bank of China helps accelerate the internationalization of RMB, take up a better position in the international market of digital currencies, and enhance cooperation in regional financial markets, to crackdown financial corruption, money laundering, tax escape, financing for terrorists and other illegal activities. China should promote the legislation of digital currency and improve relevant technologies to multiply application scenarios, paving the way for official issuance of the digital RMB.

1.3.6 Financial Regulation on Big FinTech Platforms

On September 13, 2020, the State Council issued the *Decision on the Implementation of Administration of the Market Access for Financial Holding Companies*, which stated that the People's Bank of China is appointed to issue licenses to qualified financial holding companies. On the same day, the People's Bank of China released the *Regulations on Financial Holding Companies (Trial)*, explaining the requirements and processes of market access for financial holding companies in details. Both documents came in force on November 1, 2020.

Comments: The introduction of the regulations on financial holding companies is in accordance with the supply side structural reform in financial sector, aiming to provide better services to the real economy and reduce risks in key areas accurately and effectively. With the release of the two documents, the institutional framework on the supervision of financial holding companies was initially established, measures on the isolation of risks were strengthened, and related transactions were standardized.

1.3.7 Adjustment of the Upper Interest Rate of Private Lending

On August 20, 2020, the Supreme People's Court issued the newly revised *Provisions of the Supreme People's Court on Several Issues Concerning the Applicable Law of Hearing Private Lending Cases*, which significantly lowered the upper limit of private lending interest rate to four times of the one-year LPR, replacing the original provisions of "two lines and three sections based on 24% and 36%"

Comments: The adjustment of the upper limit of private lending interest rate with judicial protection not only standardized private lending activities, but also had a far-reaching impact on the whole financial market. On the one side, it could reduce the financing costs for SMEs and help them cope with the impacts from the pandemic. On the other side, the adjustment of private lending interest rate would change the pricing mechanism of private lending market, and then standardize the businesses of Internet lending and joint lending.

1.3.8 New Regulation on Small Online Lending

On November 2, 2020, the China Banking and Insurance Regulatory Commission and the People's Bank of China jointly issued the *Interim Measures for the Administration of Online Small Loans (Draft for Comments)* to regulate the online small loans in terms of business access, business scope and basic rules, operation and management, and legal obligations.

Comments: The new regulation on small online lending emphasizes the principle of borrower protection, raises the capital threshold of small online lenders, places restrictions on their business scope, prohibits cross-provincial businesses, restrains joint loans and financing leverage of small online lenders. The new regulation furthermore standardizes small online lenders' businesses, unifies the supervision rules and operation rules, and promotes the healthy development of small online lending. The introduction of the new regulation will push the whole industry to further adjustment, large platforms to develop on resources and capital advantages, while small and medium-sized platforms may be eliminated by marketforces.

1.3.9 The Law on Commercial Banks Revised for a Third Time

On October 16, 2020, the People's Bank of China issued the

Law of the People's Republic of China on Commercial Banks (Draft for Comments). The major amendments include: to expand the subject of law application, to establish a classified access and differentiated regulatory mechanism, to improve the corporate governance of commercial banks, to improve the risk disposal and withdrawal mechanism, to adjust the operating rules of commercial banks, and to regularize the protection of customers' legal interests.

Comments: The *Law of the People's Republic of China on Commercial Banks* was issued in 1995, and was revised in 2003 and 2015 respectively. However, with the rapid development of China's banking industry, especially the continuous emergence of innovative and cross-section financial services and the extensive application of financial technology, legislation and supervision are confronted with new problems, which calls for urgent revision of the current law at that time. According to the revised law, the role of rural commercial banks and urban commercial banks is restated to conduct businesses and provide financial services within the locality where they were registered, and cannot extend businesses to other places without permission. The implementation of the revised law will further regulate the online lending and discourage small and medium-sized regional banks to operate across-region business through online lending.

1.3.10 Ant Group's Initial Public Offering Suspended

FinTech giant Ant Group's initial public offering (IPO) in both Shanghai and Hong Kong was due on November 5, 2020. However, two days before that, on November 3, the Shanghai Stock Exchange and the Hong Kong Stock Exchange released news almost at the same time that Ant Group's A share listing and H share listing were suspended. Meanwhile, the supervision authorities had talks with Ant Group, asking them to rectify their problems in financial activities, so as to make sure they operate by law, innovate with integrity and develop soundly.

Comments: In recent years, with the rapid development of FinTech innovation and financial industry, the supervision authorities have also accelerated the establishment and improvement of the financial regulatory system, issuing relevant regulatory policies, and setting up an inclusive, innovative and prudent supervision environment, which all contribute to the balance between financial development, stability and security. The suspension of Ant Group's IPO plan shows the determination of the regulators to strengthen supervision, safeguard financial stability and protect the rights and interests of investors. In the short term, tight supervision causes pain to the industry, but in the long term, it will benefit the development of the industry, and is in favor of institutions with sound system and standardized operation in the market competition.

2
Introduction to the FinTech FIRE Index

2.1 The FinTech FIRE Index

According to the definition of FinTech and the characteristics of development of China's FinTech industry, the research group designed an evaluation index system for the development of FinTech in China, namely the "FIRE" index system. The "FIRE" index refers to four first-level indicators affecting FinTech, which are Factors, Intelligence, Resources and Enterprises.

"Factors" is one of the first-level indicators, under which there are two second-level indicators and six third-level indicators, investigating factors affecting financial development in different cities from economic development and population factors perspectives. The first-level indicator "Factors" generally indicates the economic and population factors in the development of FinTech of the region. They are the foundation elements of the development of FinTech, which seldom change in the short run.

"Intelligence" is another first-level indicator, under which there are also two second-level indicators and three third-level indicators, investigating the number of patents in universities and the human resources in FinTech enterprises. The first-level index "Intelligence" mainly measures the level of local FinTech-related research and the human resources engaged in FinTech applications, which are the driving forces of FinTech development.

"Resources" is the third first-level indicator, under which there are three second-level indicators and four third-level indicators, studying the elements that support the development of FinTech from the perspectives of policy resources, network resources and financial resources. "Resources" as one of the first-level indicators, mainly tests whether FinTech is fully supported in the region, for example, whether the local government supports it, and whether there are brisk financial demands, which gives strong backing to the development of FinTech.

"Enterprises" is the fourth first-level indicator, with two second-level indicators and eight third-level indicators, exploring enterprises in the industry chain ofFinTech from quality and quantity perspectives. The first-level indicator "Enterprises" measures the intensity and quality of FinTech-related enterprises in the local area, which are the main body of FinTech development.

The "FIRE" index comprehensively demonstrates the development of FinTech in different cities from perspectives of Factors, Intelligence, Resources and Enterprises. It is helpful to analyze the current situation, explore the causes, predict further development and provide policy recommendations.

Table 2-1 **The FinTech FIRE Index**

First-level indicators	Second-level indicators	Third-level indicators
Factors	Economic development	Economic scale
		Economic growth
		The contribution of the tertiary industry
	Population factors	Population scale
		Population growth
		Population structure
Intelligence	R&D in enterprises	the number of R&D personnel in enterprises
		the number of R&D personnel in enterprises with patent transfer permission
	Research in universities	the number of patents in universities
Resources	Policy resources	the number of incubators
		Regulatory environment and business ranking
	Network resources	the popularity of network
	Financial resources	the development of inclusive finance
Enterprises	Quantity of enterprises	the quantity of FinTech enterprises
		the frequency of investments and financing of FinTech enterprises
		the number of patent applications of FinTech enterprises
		the number of patent applications of FinTech enterprises in 2019

Continued

First-level indicators	Second-level indicators	Third-level indicators
	Quality of enterprises	the number of high-tech enterprises among FinTech enterprises
		the times of investments and financing of FinTech enterprises in and after the C round
		the times of investments and financing of FinTech enterprises led by head capital
		the number of invention patents of FinTech enterprises

Source of data: Compiled by the Fintech Research Group of the Institute of Finance and Banking, Chinese Academy of Social Sciences.

2.2 Data Sources

After evaluating the availability, integrity and sustainability of the existing data, the research group collected, sorted and processed data for each indicator accordingly. The data used here are mainly from the National Bureau of Statistics, the National Enterprise Credit Information Publicity System, the State Intellectual Property Office, the official websites of provincial and municipal people's governments, and the Wind database.

It should be mentioned here, when investigating the patent achievements and the research personnel of enterprises, the research group collected part of the data from SixLens, a domestic professional platform of intellectual property rights, thanks to which, the industry layout of FinTech and the classification of patents are carefully studied. SixLens is the first state-level industrial intellectual property operation center approved and built by the State Intellectual Property Office, and it is a new generation of big data products of intellectual property independently developed by the National Intellectual Property Big Data Industrial Application Research Base. It engages more than 300 multi-source heterogeneous data in 12 categories, including intellectual property rights, business registration, investment and financing, scientific and technological literature, and standards, and it maps a capital-talent-technology knowledge domain covering 15 billion patent-entity network data.

3
China's FinTech FIRE Index

3.1 The Index

According to the scores each investigated city got, the research group put them into five classes: the first class contains three cities with 8 scores and above, account for 5% of the total samples; the second class, five cities with scores between 7 and 8, account for 8.5%; the third class, nine cities with scores between 6 and 7, account for 15.3%; the fourth class, 17 cities with scores between 4 and 6, account for 28.8%; and the fifth class, 25 cities with scores below 4, account for 42.4%.

3.1.1 The Ranking

According to the ranking in the order of total scores (table 3 – 1), Beijing, Shanghai and Shenzhen are the top three. Beijing tops the rank thanks to its absolute strengths in Factors, Intelligence and Enterprises. Shanghai takes the second place due to its outstanding performance in Intelligence, Resources and Enterprises. Shenzhen ranks the third for its comparative advantages in Resources and Enterprises.

Table 3 – 1   **China's Fintech FIRE Index Top 50**

City	Ranking	Total Scores	Factors (scores)	Intelligence (scores)	Resources (scores)	Enterprises (scores)
Beijing	1	9.105	7.489	10.000	7.928	10.000
Shanghai	2	8.657	6.974	8.847	9.288	8.790
Shenzhen	3	8.221	6.439	8.594	7.889	8.954
Hangzhou	4	7.973	7.189	8.582	7.831	7.976
Guangzhou	5	7.682	7.062	8.636	6.928	7.803
Nanjing	6	7.352	5.895	8.665	7.485	6.943
Wuhan	7	7.175	6.171	8.107	7.849	6.458
Chengdu	8	7.108	6.956	8.041	7.239	6.414
Suzhou	9	6.628	5.181	6.562	6.875	7.118
Xi'an	10	6.520	6.001	7.995	6.946	5.386
Tianjin	11	6.281	5.729	7.827	5.522	5.956
Hefei	12	6.265	5.756	7.718	5.949	5.672
Chongqing	13	6.173	6.960	7.388	5.074	5.753
Changsha	14	6.099	6.334	7.013	5.940	5.458
Jinan	15	6.077	5.505	7.376	5.252	5.983
Xiamen	16	6.031	5.885	6.737	6.034	5.587
Zhengzhou	17	6.020	5.877	6.820	6.755	4.986
Qingdao	18	5.506	5.552	5.678	6.688	4.520
Guiyang	19	5.443	4.862	5.982	7.130	4.102
Fuzhou	20	5.435	5.350	6.811	4.912	4.862
Wuxi	21	5.423	4.837	5.741	5.425	5.445
Dongguan	22	5.291	4.477	6.053	5.184	5.173
Ningbo	23	5.009	5.943	3.132	6.169	5.121
Nanchang	24	4.743	4.856	6.154	4.493	3.865

Continned

City	Ranking	TotalScores	Factors (scores)	Intelligence (scores)	Resources (scores)	Enterprises (scores)
Dalian	25	4.737	4.648	6.053	4.600	3.934
Wenzhou	26	4.717	5.433	6.215	4.511	3.488
Changzhou	27	4.707	4.346	6.047	4.754	3.871
Shenyang	28	4.632	4.484	5.605	4.448	4.133
Harbin	29	4.434	4.671	6.181	3.883	3.477
Foshan	30	4.351	5.604	3.171	5.011	4.184
Kunming	31	4.323	4.837	5.524	4.006	3.470
Shijiazhuang	32	4.266	5.306	6.029	3.483	3.120
Quanzhou	33	4.206	4.797	5.884	3.570	3.210
Nanning	34	4.021	4.805	5.227	3.601	3.124
Changchun	35	3.966	3.678	5.435	3.822	3.144
Nantong	36	3.826	4.401	3.228	4.418	3.585
Haikou	37	3.740	4.613	4.694	3.402	2.926
Yantai	38	3.700	4.335	5.250	3.704	2.317
Jiaxing	39	3.651	4.444	2.600	4.093	3.746
Taiyuan	40	3.638	4.525	4.759	3.124	2.825
Lanzhou	41	3.554	4.192	4.891	3.232	2.555
Luoyang	42	3.429	4.713	4.299	3.196	2.425
Urumchi	43	3.418	4.424	3.832	3.056	2.949
Yangzhou	44	3.321	4.218	3.127	3.571	2.897
Yinchuan	45	3.229	3.613	3.216	3.085	3.177
Jinhua	46	3.126	4.475	1.966	4.024	2.736
Shaoxing	47	3.056	4.381	2.189	3.626	2.700
Weifang	48	3.032	3.842	4.108	3.196	1.799
Xuzhou	49	2.918	4.536	2.064	3.231	2.612
Taizhou	50	2.853	3.896	2.226	4.018	2.020

Source of data: Calculated by the Fintech Research Group of the Institute of Finance and Banking, Chinese Academy of Social Sciences.

Hangzhou and Guangzhou rank fourth and fifth, with similar index values. Hangzhou is better than Guangzhou in terms of Resources, while Guangzhou is better than Hangzhou in Intelligence. Nanjing, Wuhan, Chengdu, Suzhou and Xi'an are the rest of the top 10 in order. Among them, Nanjing is strong in Intelligence, especially in scientific research of universities, but it scores moderately in Factors. Wuhan has certain advantages in Resources and university research potential of Intelligence. Chengdu performs averagely in the four fields with relatively noticeable scores in Factors and Resources. Suzhou is strong in Enterprises, but weak in Factors. Xi'an is comparatively strong in Resources and Intelligence, but weak in Enterprises.

3.1.2 Regional Distribution

From the distribution of the top 50 in the eastern, central, western and northeastern regions (Graph 3 - 1), the east outperforms the others. As for the cities of the first and second classes, six of them are in the east, two are in the central and western regions respectively. Among the cities of the third class, there are four in the eastern region, three in the central region and two in the western region.

From the perspective of north-south differences, there is an obvious north-south gap in the ranking (Graph 3 - 2). Among the cities ranking in the first and second classes, seven of them are located in the south, while only one in the north. As for the cities of the third class, five are southern cities and four are in the north.

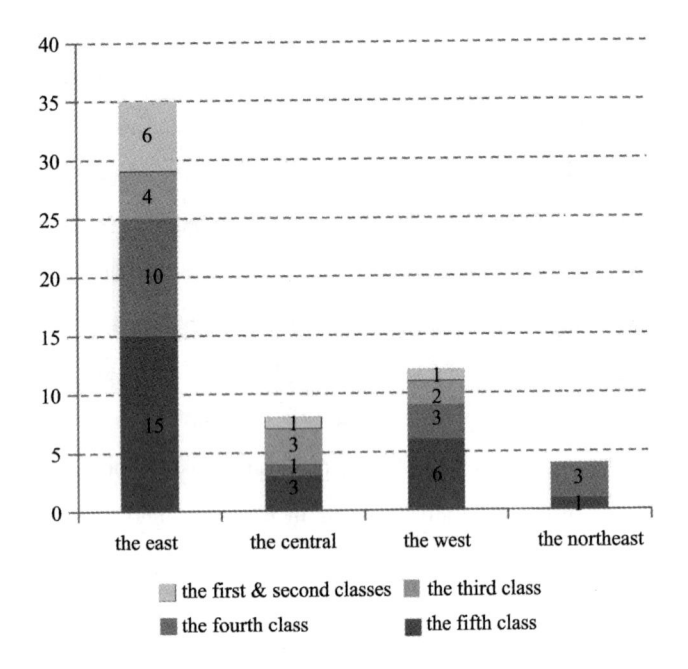

Graph 3 – 1: Regional Distribution of the Top 50 (in the four regions)

Source of data: Calculated by the Fintech Research Group of the Institute of Finance and Banking, Chinese Academy of Social Sciences.

From the perspective of city clusters, the Yangtze River Delta city cluster is an outstanding performer. Among the cities of the first and second classes, there are three cities from this area, Shanghai ranking the 2nd, Hangzhou the 4th and Nanjing the 6th. The Guangdong-Hong Kong-Macao Greater Bay Area takes up two places, with Shenzhen and Guangzhou in the 3rd and 5th places respectively. The rest of cities of the first and second classes go to cities in the Beijing-Tianjin-Hebei city cluster, the middle reaches of the Yangtze River city cluster and the Chengdu-Chongqing city cluster.

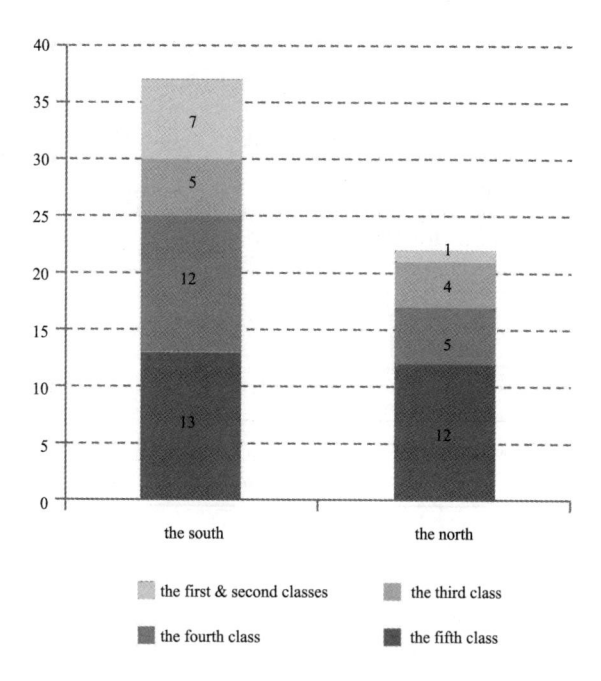

**Graph 3-2: Regional Distribution of the Top 50
(in the south and the north)**

Source of data: Calculated by the Fintech Research Group of the Institute of Finance and Banking, Chinese Academy of Social Sciences.

3.2　The Four Sub-indexes

3.2.1　Factors

As is shown in Table 3-2, the ranking is made based on the sub-index of Factors. Beijing leads the chart by its obvious superiority in economy and population. Hangzhou ranks the second with its advantages in demographic dividend, especially in population increase. Guangzhou takes the third place in the chart, followed by Shanghai, whose rank drops two places compared with that of Table 3 – 2, because of its slowing population growth. Chongqing ranks the fifth, thanks to its absolute strength in human capital. Chengdu, Shenzhen, Changsha, Wuhan and Xi'an take the places from 6 to 10, for their potential in economic and population growth.

Table 3 – 2 **Top 10 in the perspective of Factors**

	Economic factors (ranking)	Population factors (ranking)	Factors (ranking)	FIRE (ranking)
Beijing	1	3	1	1
Hangzhou	8	2	2	4
Guangzhou	3	4	3	5
Shanghai	2	6	4	2
Chongqing	18	1	5	13
Chengdu	4	5	6	8
Shenzhen	6	9	7	3
Changsha	9	10	8	14
Wuhan	7	15	9	7
Xi'an	12	13	10	10

Note: The economic factors include economic scale, growth rate and the proportion of the tertiary industry. The population factors include population scale, growth rate and structure.

Source of data: Calculated by theFintech Research Group of the Institute of Finance and Banking, Chinese Academy of Social Sciences.

In terms of regional distribution, there are still gaps between eastern, western and the central regions (Graph 3 – 3). As for the cities in the first and second classes, five of them are eastern cities, one is a central city and two are western cities. When it comes to the differences between the south and the north, cities in the south outperform those in the north (Graph 3 – 4). Among the cities sorted to the first and second classes, only Beijing is in the north, while southern cities take up the rest seven places. Within the third class of cities, six are in the south, and three are in the

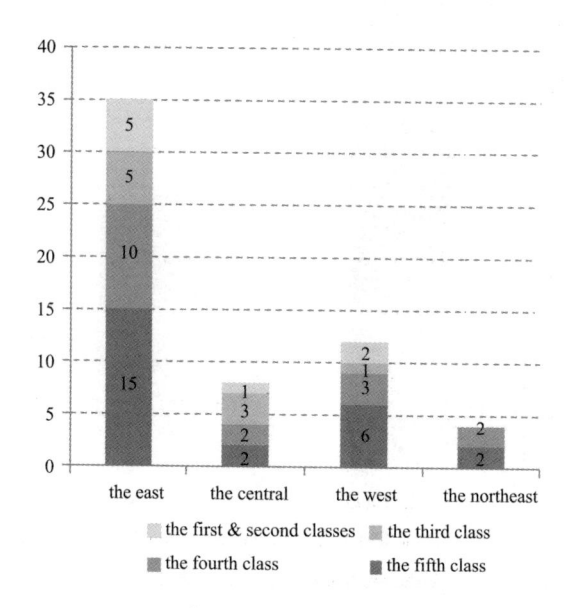

Graph 3 – 3 Regional distribution of the top 10 in the perspective of Factors (the four regions)

Source of data: Calculated by theFintech Research Group of the Institute of Finance and Banking, Chinese Academy of Social Sciences.

north. From the perspective of city clusters, as cities of the first and second classes, Hangzhou and Shanghai belong to the Yangtze River Delta city cluster, Guangzhou and Shenzhen belong to the Guangdong-Hong Kong-Macao Greater Bay Area, Chengdu and Chongqing belong to the Chengdu-Chongqing city cluster, Beijing belongs to the Beijing-Tianjin-Hebei city cluster and Changsha belongs to the middle reaches of the Yangtze River city cluster.

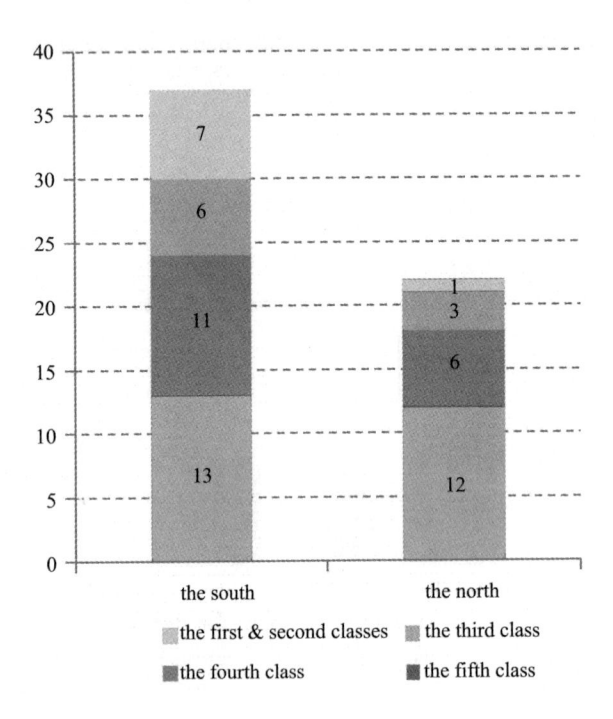

Graph 3-4 Regional distribution of the top 10 in the perspective of Factors (the south and the north)

Source of data: Calculated by theFintech Research Group of the Institute of Finance and Banking, Chinese Academy of Social Sciences.

3.2.2 Intelligence

The ranking in accordance with the sub-index Intelligence is shown in Table 3. Beijing has an absolute advantage in both R&D of enterprises and research of universities, which makes it the first in the ranking. Shanghai, Nanjing, Guangzhou and Shenzhen are the rest of the top 5 in order. Among them, Shanghai is comparatively competitive in R&D of enterprises, Nanjing is relatively strong in University research universities, Guangzhou is in favor of research in both universities and enterprises, while Shenzhen is noticeable in enterprise R&D, but weak in research of universities. Hangzhou takes the 6th place with its balanced strength in both of the two aspects. Wuhan, Chengdu, Xi'an and Tianjin take the places from 7 to 10 in order for their comprehensive research strength in the two sectors.

In terms of the regional distribution of the ranks based on Intelligence, cities in the east outnumber those in the rest of China (Graph 3 – 5). For cities of the first and second classes, the east takes up six places, the central region takes up one place and the west takes up one place as well. Whereas among cities graded in the third class, six are in the east, three in the central region, and two in the west. From the perspective of north-and-south, southern cities are still preponderate (Graph 3 – 6). Seven southern cities are graded as first and second classes, while only one city in the north is graded in the same class. Besides, as for cities of the third class, the south takes up five places, and the north takes up four. From the perspective of city clusters, three cities in the Yangtze River Delta are graded in the first two classes, two cities in the Guangdong-Hong Kong-Macao Greater Bay Area are graded in these two classes, and one city in the Beijing-Tianjin-Hebei City Cluster, one in Chengdu-Chongqing City Cluster and one in the middle reaches of the Yangtze River City Cluster are graded in the same classes.

Table 3 -3   **Top 10 in the perspective of Intelligence**

	R&D of enterprises (ranking)	Research of universities (ranking)	Intelligence (ranking)	FIRE (ranking)
Beijing	1	1	1	1
Shanghai	3	7	2	2
Nanjing	6	2	3	6
Guangzhou	5	3	4	5
Shenzhen	2	13	5	3
Hangzhou	4	6	6	4
Wuhan	10	5	7	7
Chengdu	8	9	8	8
Xi'an	13	4	9	10
Tianjin	12	8	10	11

Note: R&D of enterprises measures the intellectual contribution of local FinTech enterprises, including the total number of R&D personnel of enterprises in the city and the total number of R&D personnel of enterprises with patent transfer license. Research of universities measures the intellectual contribution of local universities to the development of FinTech, and the proxy variable is the number of patents from local universities.

Source of data: Calculated by the Fintech Research Group of the Institute of Finance and Banking, Chinese Academy of Social Sciences.

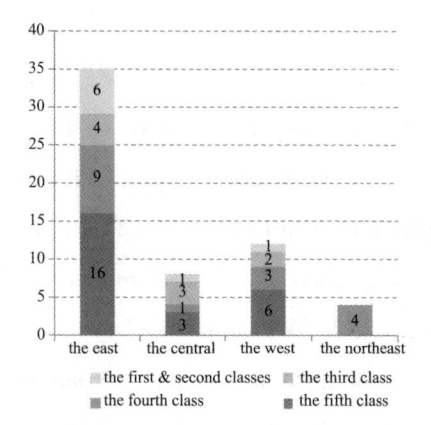

Graph 3-5: Regional distribution of the Top 10 in the perspective of Intelligence (the four regions)

Source of data: Calculated by the Fintech Research Group of the Institute of Finance and Banking, Chinese Academy of Social Sciences.

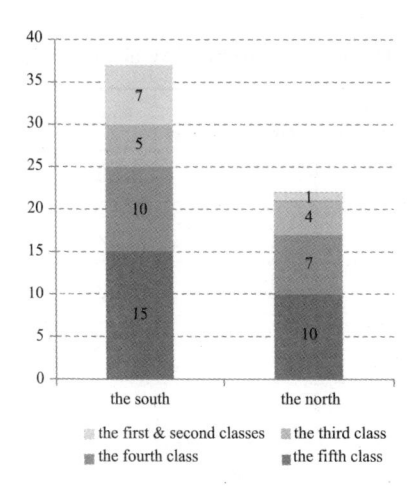

Graph 3-6: Regional distribution of the Top 10 in the perspective of Intelligence (the south and the north)

Source of data: Calculated by the Fintech Research Group of the Institute of Finance and Banking, Chinese Academy of Social Sciences.

3.2.3 Resources

Table 3-4 shows the ranking based on Resources. Shanghai takes the 1st place for its strengths in policy, network and financial resources. Beijing and Shenzhen rank the 2nd and the 3rd respectively for their merits in network and financial resources, though they are weak in policy resources. Wuhan ranks 4th in the chart, followed by Hangzhou, whose strength in network and financial resources is obvious. The next is Nanjing, which is outstanding in policy and financial resources. Chengdu, Guiyang, Xi'an and Guangzhou take the places from 7 to 10, for their overall performance in policy, network and financial resources.

Table 3-4   **Top 10 in the perspective of Resources**

	Policy resources (ranking)	Network resources (ranking)	Financial resources (ranking)	Resources (ranking)	FIRE (ranking)
Shanghai	1	2	2	1	2
Beijing	12	1	5	2	1
Shenzhen	10	3	3	3	3
Wuhan	5	7	9	4	7
Hangzhou	15	4	1	5	4
Nanjing	7	10	4	6	6
Chengdu	4	8	20	7	8
Guiyang	3	6	30	8	19

Continued

	Policy resources (ranking)	Network resources (ranking)	Financial resources (ranking)	Resources (ranking)	FIRE (ranking)
Xi'an	2	14	25	9	10
Guangzhou	16	5	7	10	5

Note: Policy resources mainly measure the local government's support for FinTech development, including the number of incubators in the city and the local regulatory and business environment. Network resources measure the attention from network on the local FinTech development. Financial resources measure the local development of inclusive finance.

Source of data: Calculated by the Fintech Research Group of the Institute of Finance and Banking, Chinese Academy of Social Sciences.

Seen from the regional distribution of the top 10 in this part, eastern cities still have evident advantages (Graph 3 – 7). Among the cities in the first and second classes, eastern cities take up five places, cities in the central region take up one and western cities take up two places. For cities of the third class, six of them are in located the east, and the rest three are in the central region. In the perspective of south-and-north, southern cities outperform their counterparts in the north (Graph 3 – 8). For cities of the first two classes in this part, six of them are situated in the south and two in the north, while for cities of the third class, southern and northern cities take up six and three places respectively. When it comes to city clusters, cities in the Yangtze River Delta still holds more places within the first and second classes, with three cities listed; while

Beijing-Tianjin-Hebei City Cluster, Guangdong-Hong Kong-Macao Greater Bay Area, the middle reaches of the Yangtze River City Cluster, Chengdu-Chongqing City Cluster and Central Guizhou City Cluster, each has one city graded in the first two classes. It is worth noting that, ten out of the top 17 cities in the perspective of Resources are in the Yangtze River Delta, thanks to their overwhelming advantages in financial resources.

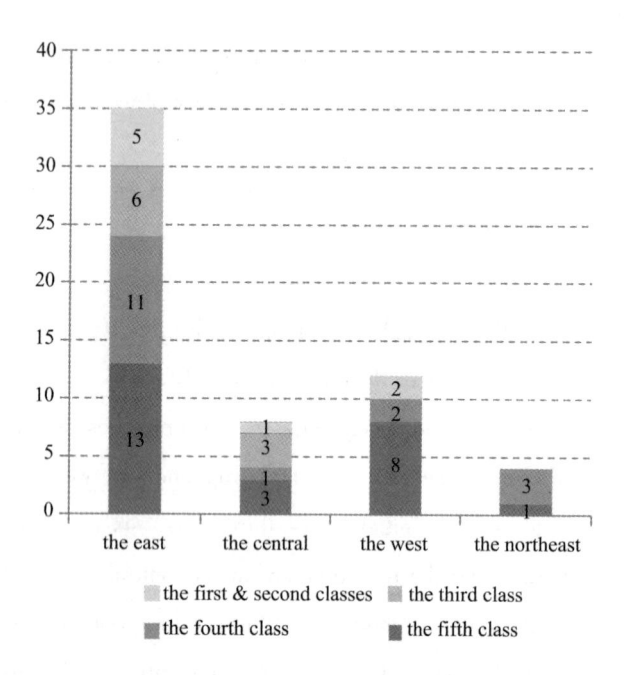

Graph 3-7: Regional distribution of the Top 10 in the perspective of Resources (the four regions)

Source of data: Calculated by the Fintech Research Group of the Institute of Finance and Banking, Chinese Academy of Social Sciences.

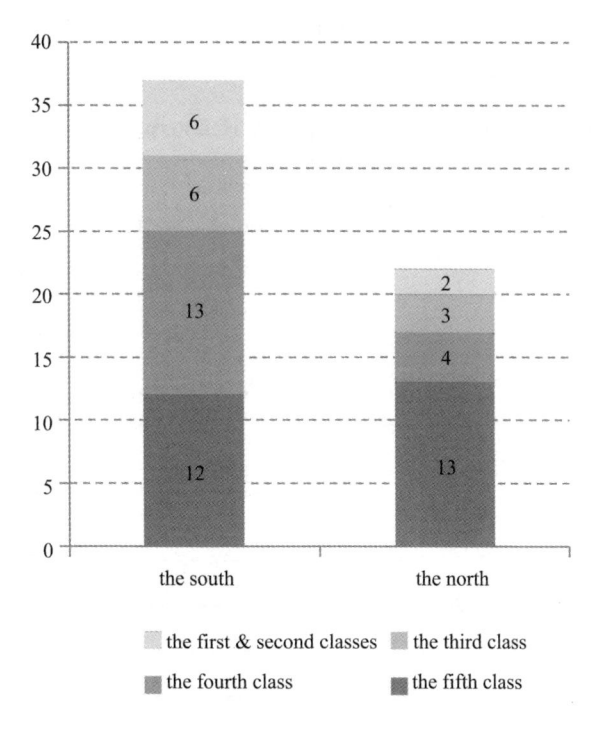

Graph 3 – 8: Regional distribution of the Top 10 in the perspective of Resources (the south and the north)

Source of data: Calculated by the Fintech Research Group of the Institute of Finance and Banking, Chinese Academy of Social Sciences.

3.2.4 Enterprises

The ranking of the top 10 in the perspective of enterprises is shown in Table 3 – 5. Beijing holds the leading position for its overwhelming superiority in both the quantity and quality of FinTech related enterprises. The next two are Shenzhen and Shanghai, also strong in both of the two aspects. Then it is Hangzhou, ranking 4th. Guangzhou, Suzhou, Nanjing, Wuhan, Chengdu and Jinan take the rest of the top 10 places in order.

Table 3 – 5 **Top 10 in the perspective of Enterprises**

	the quantity of FinTech enterprises (ranking)	the quality of FinTech enterprises (ranking)	Enterprises (ranking)	FIRE (ranking)
Beijing	1	1	1	1
Shenzhen	2	3	2	3
Shanghai	3	2	3	2
Hangzhou	4	4	4	4
Guangzhou	5	5	5	5
Suzhou	6	6	6	9
Nanjing	7	7	7	6
Wuhan	9	8	8	7
Chengdu	8	9	9	8
Jinan	13	10	10	15

Note: The quantity of FinTech enterprises evaluate the local intensity of FinTech related enterprises from the perspectives of the number of local FinTech enterprises, stages of their investment and financing, and their patent application. The quality of FinTech enterprises further inspects the intensity of high-quality FinTech enterprises in the city.

Source of data: Calculated by the Fintech Research Group of the Institute of Finance and Banking, Chinese Academy of Social Sciences.

In respect of the regional distribution of the ranking in this part, eastern cities have absolute advantages over their counterparts in the other regions (Graph 3 –9). Among the cities of the first and second classes, seven are in the east, and one is from the central region. Of the nine cities of the third class, four are in the east, two are in the central region and three are in the west. From the perspective of the south-and-north, the southern cities still outperform those in the north (Graph 3 – 10). As for cities graded in the first and second classes in the perspective of Enterprises, the south holds seven places, while the north only one place. Among the cities of the third class, six are in the south and three in the north. In terms of city clusters, the Yangtze River Delta city cluster still accounts for the majority of the first and second-class cities, taking up four places.

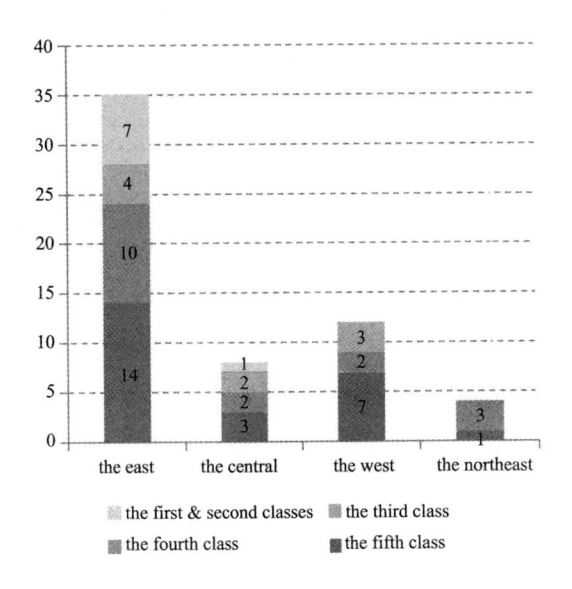

Graph 3 – 9: Regional distribution of the Top 10 in the perspective of Enterprises (the four regions)

Source of data: Calculated by the Fintech Research Group of the Institute of Finance and Banking, Chinese Academy of Social Sciences.

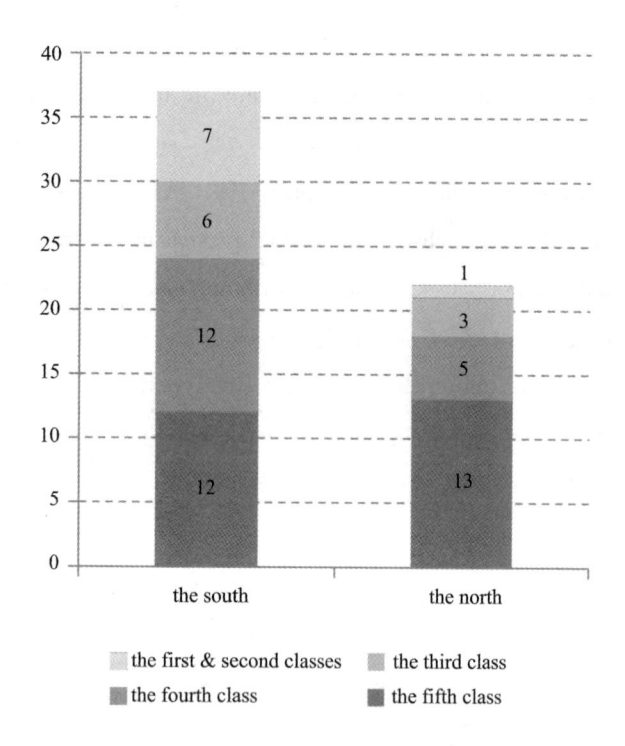

Graph 3 – 10: Regional distribution of the Top 10 in the perspective of Enterprises (the south and the north)

Source of data: Calculated by the Fintech Research Group of the Institute of Finance and Banking, Chinese Academy of Social Sciences.

4
Case Studies

After general assessment of the investigated cities, in order to fully compare them from perspectives of every sub-index and further explore the significant differences between cities of different classes in the development of FinTech, the research group conducted case studies on cities selected from each class.

4.1 The First Class: Beijing, Shanghai and Shenzhen

4.1.1 Beijing

Beijing topsChina's FinTech FIRE index with its leading position in three sub-indexes—Factors, Intelligence and Enterprises, which demonstrates that Beijing has become a prominent city with comprehensive strengths in FinTech development, setting an example for other cities.

As a matter of fact, in 2018, Beijing released the *Beijing FinTech Development Plan (2018 – 2022)*, which proposes that by the end of 2022, there should be five to ten internationally renowned

FinTech enterprises, three to five innovation clusters with international influence, and 10 to 15 major application projects for demonstration. So far, Beijing has achieved initial success in the development of FinTech, especially when it comes to the ranking from the perspectives of the sub-indexes—Intelligence and Enterprises—and their three levels of indicators, where Beijing all takes the first place, which shows that it has acquired a sound development in both the supply and demand sides of the industry chain of FinTech. Therefore, a pleasant environment is taking shape, where innovation drives research and development, research and development facilitate technologies, and technologies enables scenarios.

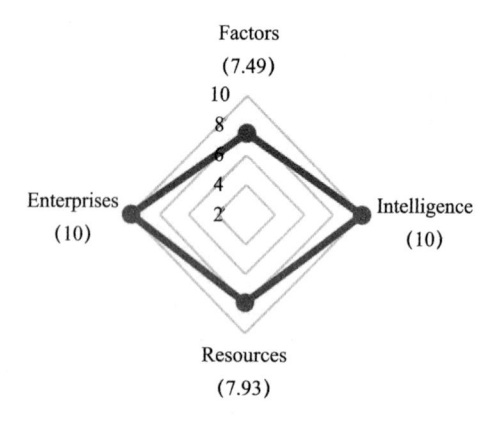

4 – 1 Bejing's FIRE Index(scores)

4.1.2 Shanghai

Shanghai ranks the 2nd in China's FinTech FIRE index. For its rankings in the perspectives of the four sub-indexes, that of

Resources is the most remarkable, where Shanghai takes the 1st place, while those of Factors, Intelligence and Enterprises are ranked the 2nd, 3rd and 5th respectively. In general, Shanghai is a traditional international financial center with relatively full-featured financial market and developed systems, where financial institutions and elements are clustered, and the development of FinTech driven by the application scenarios at the demand side is its distinctive feature.

At the beginning of 2020, Shanghai issued an implementation plan to accelerate the construction of the Shanghai FinTech Center, promoting the research and development of FinTech, boosting the agglomeration of the FinTech industry, creating pilots of regulatory innovation and a first-class environment for FinTech development. By now, FinTech in Shanghai is growing with distinct characteristics. According to the rankings of the third-level indicators, business environment in Shanghai is the best of all, while inclusive finance, the quantity of FinTech enterprises and stages of financing and investments in Shanghai all take the 2nd places in the corresponding charts, which suggests that Shanghai is highly market-oriented, where there is sophisticated financial infrastructure and financial institutions are favored by capital. In contrast, Shanghai ranks slightly lower in terms of Intelligence, especially in patent applications by universities, ranking 7th in the chart, which indicates that research and development related to FinTech needs to be strengthened.

42　National Think Tank

```
                    Factors
                    (6.97)
                      10
                       8
                       6
    Enterprises        4          Intelligence
     (8.79)            2            (8.85)


                    Resources
                     (9.29)
```

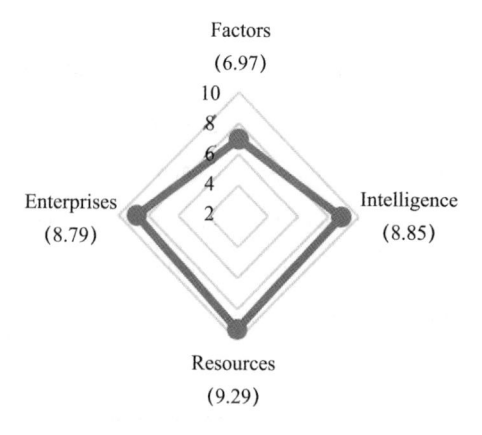

4－2　Shanghai's FIRE Index(scores)

4.1.3　Shenzhen

Shenzhen ranks 3rd in China's FinTech FIRE index, while when it comes to the sub-indexes, it takes the 2nd place, the 3rd place and again the 3rd place in the rankings from the perspectives of Enterprises, Resources and Intelligence respectively. In general, among the top three cities, Shenzhen does not have strength in terms of population size, but numerous technology enterprises there have attracted a large number of research personnel and generated multiple high-quality innovative achievements, which promotes the development of FinTech in Shenzhen greatly. It reflects that FinTech in Shenzhen holds its leading position in technological innovation, due to its high density of technological innovation enterprises and high conversion rate of research achievements.

In the middle of 2020, in order to implement the *Opinions on Finance Support the Construction of the Guangdong- Hong Kong-*

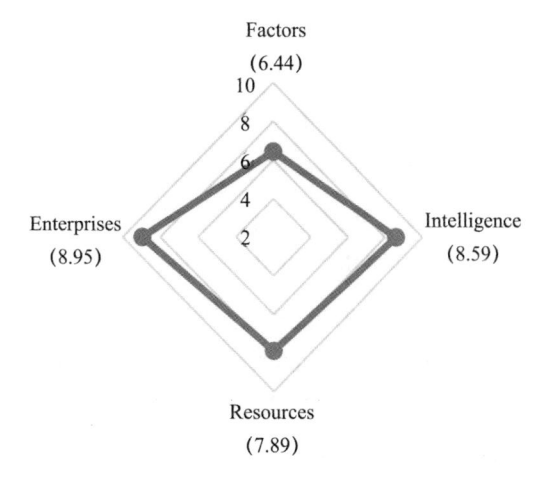

```
           Factors
           (6.44)
           10
            8
            6
            4
Enterprises              Intelligence
 (8.95)     2              (8.59)


           Resources
            (7.89)
```

4 – 3 Shenzhen's FIRE Index(scores)

Macao Greater Bay Area issued by the People's Bank of China and other four departments, Shenzhen government formulated the *Shenzhen Implementation Action Plan*, and proposed to build two financial centers, namely, the global FinTech center and the global sustainable financial center. In recent years, more than one important FinTech institution has settled in Shenzhen, including the FinTech Research Institute of the Digital Currency Research Institute of the People's Bank of China, the Institute for Future Financial RegTech, and Baihang Credit (the only market-oriented personal credit investigation agency in China), making Shenzhen outstanding in FinTech-related technologies and infrastructure. According to the rankings, Shenzhen is strong in Enterprises. Though it cannot compete with Shanghai in the number of FinTech enterprises and their stages of financing and investment, Shenzhen still overtakes Shanghai to take the 2nd place in the ranking from the perspective of Enterprises for its numerous patents from enterprises. However, Shenzhen is no better than Shanghai in university research, ranking 13th in the chart.

Generally speaking, the top three cities of the first class are distinctive in their own development. Beijing is superior in almost every aspect for the concentration of elements like regulation, universities, internet and financial institutions, as a result of early planning. Shanghai takes the 2nd place for abundant financial resources. Shenzhen ranks 3rd, thanks to its magnet for technology enterprises.

4.2 The Second Class: Hangzhou, Guangzhou and Chengdu

4.2.1 Hangzhou

Hangzhou ranks 4th in China's FinTech FIRE index, leading the second class of cities. As for the rankings from the four perspectives, Hangzhou takes the 2nd place in the perspective of Factors, the 4th in Enterprises, the 5th in Resources, the 6th in Intelligence. As one of the new first-tier cities, it has witnessed remarkable achievements in the development of digital economy, attracting a large number of populations. Meanwhile, Ant Group, Hang Seng Electronics, and other emerging large FinTech enterprises are located here, so Hangzhou's R&D capacity and professional human resources are among the tops in China.

```
            Factors
            (7.19)
              10
               8
               6
Enterprises    4    Intelligence
  (7.98)       2      (8.58)

            Resources
             (7.83)
```

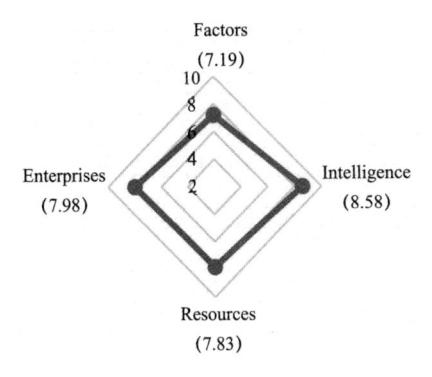

4 – 4 Hangzhou's FIRE Index(scores)

In May 2019, Hangzhou government released the *Hangzhou Special Plan for the Construction of an International FinTech Center*, aiming to build a leading city of FinTech in China and a global FinTech Application and Innovation Center in the world, with the promotion of FinTech-related research and innovation, infrastructure construction, industrial application and policy support. It is clearly shown by the rankings that the implementation of the special plan in Hangzhou has achieved effective results. For one thing, its inclusive finance is the best developed in China, which reflects its great strengths in financial infrastructure construction and the accessibility of financial services. This is not only the result of the development of FinTech, but also the foundation for further development of FinTech. For another, its numbers of research personnel and patents from enterprises are among the tops, and its investment and financing activities are also among the most active, which demonstrates that Hangzhou is fruitful in technology application and quite attractive to the capital market, boosting the agglomeration of FinTech-related elements. However, the number of incubators in Hangzhou is not that large because the local FinTech industry is relatively sophisticated with a high threshold. In the future, more attention should be paid to the support and guidance of start-ups to enhance healthy competition within the industry.

4.2.2 Guangzhou

Guangzhou ranks 5th in China's FinTech FIRE index. As for the rankings from the four perspectives, it takes the 3rd place in the perspective of Factors, the 4th in Intelligence, the 5th in Enterprises, and the 10th in Resources. As a traditional first-tier city, Guangzhou is developed in economy and is an important component of the Pearl River Delta and the Greater Bay Area, which makes it superior in the development of FinTech industry. According to the rankings of the three levels of indicators, FinTech in Guangzhou is generating strong momentum.

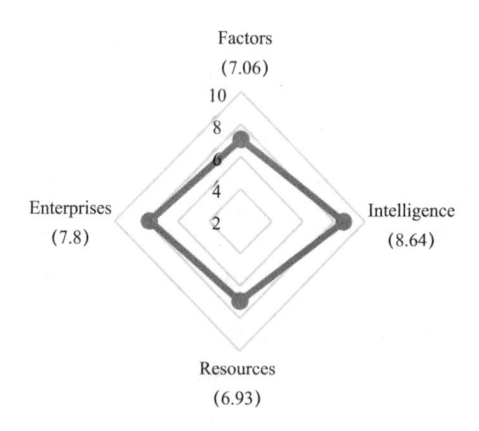

4-5 Guangzhou's FIRE Index(scores)

- Factors (7.06)
- Intelligence (8.64)
- Resources (6.93)
- Enterprises (7.8)

As early as October 2018, the Financial Affairs Bureau of Guangzhou Municipality issued the *Opinions on the Implementation of Promoting the Innovation and Development of FinTech in Guangzhou*, encouraging financial institutions to strengthen cooperation with technology enterprises, to set up different financial business scenarios, and establish distinctive FinTech modes in various financial fields including industrial finance and green finance. In October 2020, the preparations for China's fifth futures exchange in Guangzhou have also come to the final stage. The carbon emission is the first variety, showing Guangzhou's outstanding innovation and strong research capacity in the development of FinTech. Besides, its rankings in the three-level rankings also illustrate its strength in research and innovation, as it takes the 2nd place in the ranking of the quantity of high-tech enterprises and the 3rd place of the number of patents from universities. Whereas, Guangzhou is no better than Hangzhou in the ranking of the number of incubators, which suggests that start-ups should be further encouraged and supported.

4.2.3 Chengdu

Chengdu ranks 8th in China's FinTech FIRE index, the last one of the second class, and the only one from the west in the first two classes. As for the rankings from the four perspectives, it takes the 6th place in the perspective of Factors, the 7th in Resources, the 8th in Intelligence, and the 9th in Enterprises. As the top city in western China, Chengdu should attribute its development in FinTech to its economic and population scale, the investment of government resources, and the increasing and upgrading of FinTech enterprises.

```
                Factors
                (6.96)
                 10
                  8
                  6
                  4
Enterprises          Intelligence
  (6.41)    2         (8.04)

                Resources
                 (7.24)
```

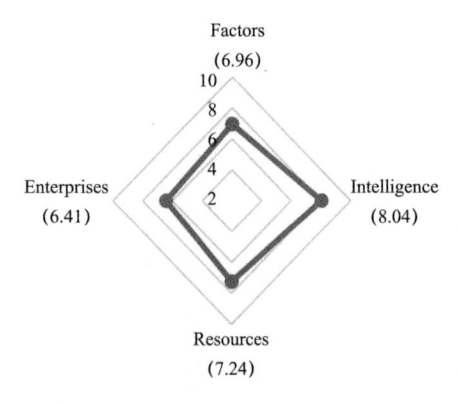

4-6　Chengdu's FIRE Index(scores)

In May 2020, Chengdu government, together with the Chengdu Branch of People's Bank of China, issued a FinTech development plan, which is the first in China that is jointly issued by the local government and the People's Bank of China. The plan states to build Chengdu into a regional FinTech center with international influence by 2022. To jointly release a development plan on FinTech with the regulator, Chengdu government is ingenious and innovative in managing industrial ecology and enhancing supervision. According to the rankings by the third-level index, its quantity of incubators is the fifth largest in China, its quantity of high-tech enterprises the seventh largest, and its number of patents also the seventh largest, showing that the development of the local FinTech industry is vibrant and energetic. However, Chengdu ranks lower in terms of the development of inclusive finance and the stages of financing (especially C round financing), which indicates that local FinTech enterprises are still at a start-up stage, and the financial infrastructure needs further

4.3 The Third Class: Suzhou and Zhengzhou

4.3.1 Suzhou

Suzhou ranks 9th in China's FinTech FIRE index, top of the third-class cities. As for the rankings from the four perspectives, it takes the 6th place in the perspective of Enterprises, the 11th in Resources, the 18th in Intelligence, and the 23rd in Factors. The total industrial growth in Suzhou has already exceeds that of Shanghai, making Suzhou the largest industrial city in China, where the system of manufacturing is one of the most sophisticated, laying sound foundation for the development of economy. The state strategic pilot programs of SME digital credit reporting, digital currency and FinTech innovative supervision were all launched in Suzhou, revealing its great potential and merits in the development of the FinTech industry.

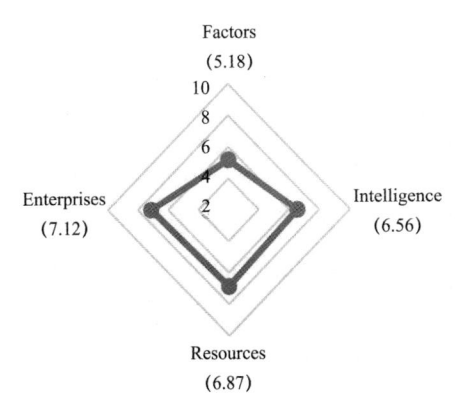

4-7 Suzhou's FIRE Index(scores)

In the rankings of the third-level index, Suzhou is in the front in terms of FinTech related indicators; for example, it ranks 6th in the ranking of C round financing and that of the number of patents from FinTech enterprises, and it ranks 7th in the ranking of the quantity of research personnel, which shows its tremendous strength in the emerging industry as a traditional industrial city. What makes Suzhou not that outstanding in the overall ranking is the growth of economy and population, the contribution of tertiary industry and the number of patents from the universities. Considering that Suzhou being deeply engaged in industry for a long time, its basic economic pattern is unlikely to change greatly in the short run. Suzhou should make efforts in attracting FinTech related talents, encouraging more investments in FinTech related theoretical research and major projects, and promoting the efficient transformation of scientific research achievements.

4.3.2 Zhengzhou

Zhengzhou ranks 17th in China's FinTech FIRE index, the last one in the third-class cities. As for the rankings from the four perspectives, it takes the 12th place in the perspective of Resources, the 14th in Factors, the 15th in Intelligence, and the 20th in Enterprises. Among cities ranked in the third class, its strength in Resources is obvious, while it is weak in Enterprises, though the number of incubators is impressive, which indicates that initial development has achieved for its policy-driven FinTech industry, but start-ups still need more capital venture for further growth.

In 2019, Zhengzhou government released the *Regulations on High-tech Business Incubators in Zhengzhou*, aiming to build an internationally competitive center for innovative start-ups in central China, by means of policy support to improve the capacity of incubation system. It is shown in this report that Zhengzhou takes the second place in the ranking of the number of incubators in China, which suggests that relevant policies have played a great role in promoting the launching of innovative start-ups in Zhengzhou. When it comes to the quality of enterprises, Zhengzhou ranks among top 10 in the number of patents from FinTech enterprises, while it ranks 30th in terms of financing of or after C round, and ranks the 21st in the investment leaded by the head capital. This reflects that the capital market is still assessing the FinTech enterprises in Zhengzhou. Therefore, Zhengzhou should make efforts in capital attracting, bridging the gap between FinTech enterprises and the capital market, especially the equity investment market, giving full play to the incentive mechanism of benefit sharing and risk sharing.

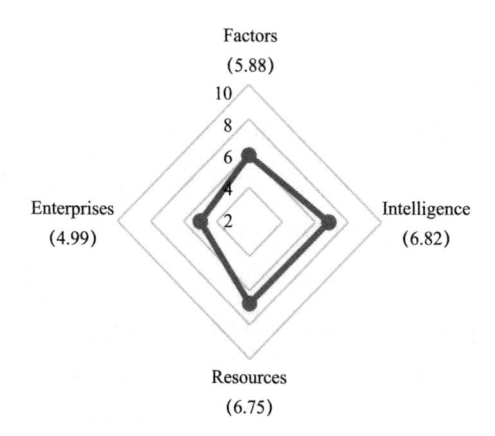

4-8 Zhengzhou's FIRE Index(scores)

4.4 The Fourth Class: Guiyang and Foshan

4.4.1 Guiyang

Guiyang ranks 19th in China's FinTech FIRE index, next to Qingdao. As for the rankings from the four perspectives, it takes the 24th place in the perspective of Factors, the 25th in Enterprises, the 26th in Intelligence, while it is worth noting that thanks to its status as a national center for big data and preferential policies from the central government, Guiyang ranks the 8th in terms of Resources. Located in the southwest of China, Guiyang is the political, economic, cultural, educational and traffic center of Guizhou Province, and also an important transportation and communication hub as well as industrial base, business center and tourist attraction in the southwestern region. According to the rankings of the second-level indictors, its rankings in political resources and network resources are the 3rd and the 6th respectively, which is also a reason why it ranks among the top 10 in terms of Resources.

In recent years, Guiyang often comes into the spotlight together with FinTech, because of the sound development of the big data industry there. As a comprehensive national pilot area of big data, Guiyang has made great achievements in the construction and development of the big data industry. In addition, Guiyang has strengthened the system construction and talent training mechanism for the big data industry, releasing the first local laws and regulations on big data security in China. Moreover, according to the rankings of the third-level indicators, Guiyang ranks 18th in terms of financing after C round, reflecting that the development of FinTech enterprises in Guiyang has reached a certain level and the relevant industrial chain tends to be stable.

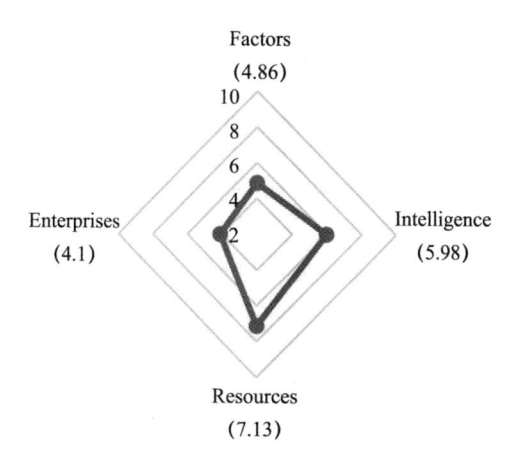

4-9 Guiyang's FIRE Index(scores)

4.4.2 Foshan

Foshan ranks 30th in China's FinTech FIRE index, the middle of the investigated cities. As for the rankings from the four perspectives, it takes the 17th place in the perspective of Factors, the 23rd in Enterprises, the 23rd in Resources, and the 43rd in Intelligence. In the rankings of the second-level indicators, it ranks 27th in terms of the quantity of research personnel, while the 44th in university research, which is the reason for its place in Intelligence. Foshan is an important manufacturing base in China and even the world. It is the 17th in China with a GDP of over one trillion, where the economic development is vibrant and the R&D driven by enterprises' own production demands is of high level. According to the report, Foshan is weak in the research of universities, due to the lack of top research institutions on the one hand, and the deficiency of further research in basic theories and key technologies on the other.

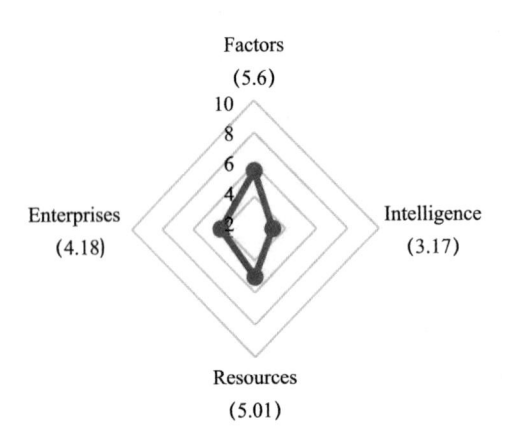

Factors
(5.6)

Enterprises
(4.18)

Intelligence
(3.17)

Resources
(5.01)

4 – 10 Bejing's FIRE Index(scores)

Since 2011, Foshan has taken the integration of finance, technology and industry as its developing strategy, and released many a policy and measure to promote the integration of technology and finance to support industrial transformation and development. During the *13th Five-Year Plan period,* Foshan has made great achievements in the allocation of financial resources to the field of science and technology, the transformation of scientific and technological achievements and the development of emerging industries. As is stated in this report, the number of FinTech enterprises and the total number of patents from FinTech enterprises in Foshan both rank 23rd in the rankings, and the number of high-tech enterprises among FinTech enterprises ranks 20th, which suggests the integration of finance, technology and industry in Foshan has achieved effective results. In the future, Foshan should promote the integration of research, finance, technology and industry with the help of local research force and introduc research teams, so as to improve the development of FinTech in the city.

4.5　The Fifth Class

There are 25 cities ranked in the fifth class in this report, accounting for 42.4% of the total. FinTech in these cities is less developed, so it needs all-round improvement. As the cities in this class are quite different in influence factors, they are not analyzed in this report.

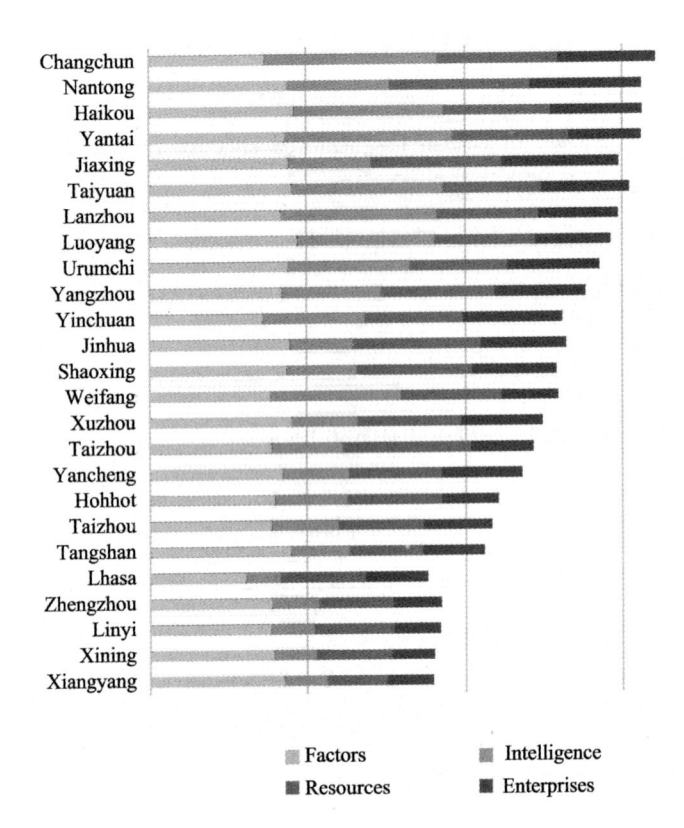

4-11 The FIRE Index of cities of the fifth class

5
Distribution Characteristics of FinTech in Cities and Industrial Chains

This report defines FinTech in a broad sense, referring to both the financial services that technological companies are engaged in and the advanced technologies used by traditional financial institutions. According to the Investment and Financing Intelligence System from SixLens (Box 5), this report selected 25 items related to FinTech, including cloud computing, blockchain, big data, machine learning, Internet platform, smart finance, monetary and financial services. Meanwhile, the positions of FinTech enterprises in the FinTech industrial chain are designated with the chain of "fundamental technology research and development—technology integration output—financial scenario construction". For instance, in this report, companies that provide big data, blockchain and cloud computing are classified as the upstream of the FinTech industrial chain, those provide Internet security services are classified as the midstream, and those provide monetary and financial services are sorted in the downstream. Companies in the upstream are strongest in technology, those in the downstream are strongest in financial services, while those in the midstream are moderate in both.

Box 5

As a business investigation tool for scientific and technological information, the global Patent Investment and Financing Intelligence System is developed by the National Intellectual Property Big Data Industrial Application Research Base (SixLens) with its self-developed global scientific and technological competition and cooperation knowledge graph database and other technologies, such as big data, artificial intelligence, and knowledge graph. Its key part consists of 40 million enterprises, 15 thousand investment institutions, 23 million inventor engineers connected by 130 million full-cycle patents data and multi-source heterogeneous data resources such as the full amount of scientific and technological literature and standard statistics. It generates 1.7 billion pieces of competition and cooperation graph data through data processing, to assist governments, investment institutions, banks, bonding companies, insurance agencies, trading institutions and large enterprises to evaluate the technological value of technology enterprises and identify associated risks behind patens, from a panoramic and scientific view.

Source of data: SixLens website.

Table 5 – 1 **Positions of the 25 items in the industrial chain**

Industrial Chain	Items
Bottom R&D (upstream of the industrial chain)	Cloud computing, blockchain, big data, machine learning, deep learning, knowledge graph, man-machine interaction
Technology integration output (midstream of the industrial chain)	Internet service, internet platforms, basic software development, APP development, network and information security software development, internet security service, information system integration service, information processing and storage service, IT consulting service

Continued

Industrial Chain	Items
Financial scenarios construction (downstream of the industrial chain)	Smart finance, car rental, automobile finance, finance, monetary and financial service, capital market service, rental service, insurance

Note: These 25 items are from SixLens' global patent Investment and Financing Intelligence System.

5.1 The Distribution of FinTech Enterprises

5.1.1 The Regional Distribution of FinTech Enterprises

The number of FinTech enterprises determines the regional FinTech supply capacity. There are 50,436 FinTech enterprises in the 59 cities investigated in this report. As is shown in Graph 5 – 1, among the top 20 cities in the FinTech FIRE index, Beijing takes the 1st place with 9,830 FinTech enterprises, while Shanghai (6,577), Shenzhen (6,222), Guangzhou (3,101) and Hangzhou (2,857) rank from 2nd to the 5th respectively. They are followed by Chengdu (1,937), Nanjing (1,902), Suzhou (1,763), Wuhan (1,407) and Tianjin (1,356). In terms of quantity, the numbers of FinTech enterprises in Beijing, Shanghai and Shenzhen account for 19.5%, 13.0% and 12.3% of the total respectively, indicating that the supply of FinTech in these three cities is more sufficient and the competition is fiercer than that in other cities.

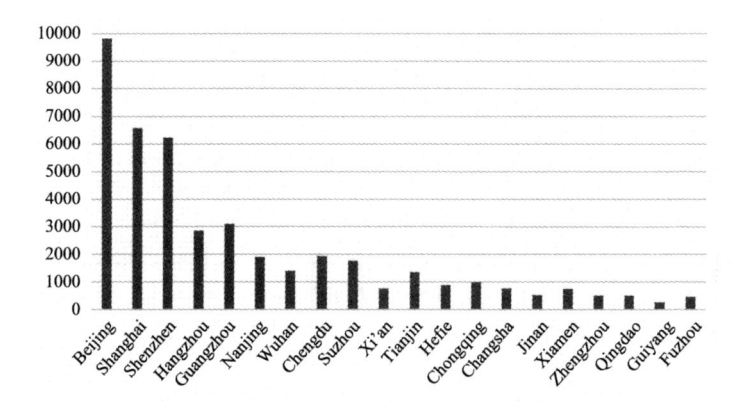

Graph 5-1: the distribution ofFinTech enterprises in the FT 20 cities

Note: FT20 cities refer to the top 20 cities in China's FinTech FIRE index

Source of data: Calculated by SixLens and the Fintech Research Group of the Institute of Finance and Banking, Chinese Academy of Social Sciences.

5.1.2 The Distribution of FinTech Enterprises in the Industrial Chain

Most FinTech enterprises are in the middle of the industrial chain, then in the upstream, and fewest in the downstream. According to statistical calculation, the average number of FinTech enterprises located in the upstream, midstream and downstream of the industrial chain in the 59 investigated cities account for 21.4%, 74.2% and 4.4%, respectively. It shows that China's FinTech enterprises focus more on the output of technology integration, but less in supply of financial services and basic research and development innovation of emerging digital technology, which is less in favor of boosting the core competitiveness of China's FinTech enterprises in the international market.

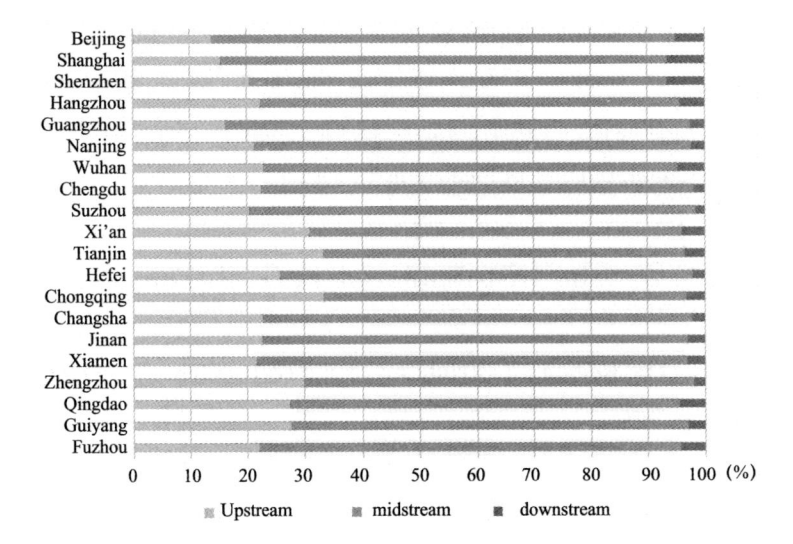

Graph 5-2: The distribution of FinTech enterprises of the FT 20 cities in the industrial chain

Source of data: Calculated by SixLens and the Fintech Research Group of the Institute of Finance and Banking, Chinese Academy of Social Sciences.

The positions of FinTech enterprises in the industrial chain are different in cities. According to Graph 5-2, among the top 20 cities in the FinTech FIRE index, Guangzhou, Beijing, Shanghai and Suzhou takes up the highest proportion of enterprises in the middle of the industrial chain, accounting for 81.3%, 81.1%, 78.0% and 77.9%, respectively. Chongqing, Tianjin, Xi'an and Zhengzhou take up the highest proportion of enterprises in the upstream of the industrial chain, accounting for 33.4%, 33.3%, 30.9% and 30.0%, respectively. Shenzhen, Shanghai, Beijing and Wuhan take up the highest proportion of enterprises in the downstream, with 6.6%, 6.5%, 5.0% and 4.8%, respectively. Moreover, among the top 5 cities with the largest number of FinTech enterprises, only Hangzhou's number of enterprises in the upstream is above the average, which is closely related to the rapid development of e-commerce and digital technology in Hangzhou.

5.2 The Distribution of FinTech Patents

5.2.1 The Regional Distribution of FinTech Patents in Quality and Quantity

Patents reflect the technological attributes ofFinTech enterprises. This report collects patents of FinTech enterprises in the 59 investigated cities to form data of patents at city level. According to Graph 5 – 3, Beijing leads the chart in quantity with 281,000 patent applications, followed by Shenzhen (147,000), Shanghai (63,000), Guangzhou (42,000) and Hangzhou (35,000). Then there are Suzhou (33,000), Chengdu (24,000), Nanjing (20,000), Jinan (19,000) and Zhengzhou (18,000) in the ranking. It can be seen that the top 10 cities in terms of the number of patent applications and the number of FinTech enterprises are similar, except Jinan and Zhengzhou.

Invention patent is the best reflection of the quality of patents. Among the top 20 cities in theFinTech FIRE index, Beijing, Zhengzhou, Hefei and Wuhan rank the top 4 with 78.9%, 75.9%, 74.8% and 73.7% of invention patents, followed by Jinan (71.9%) and Shenzhen (70.0%), and then Nanjing (69.9%) and Shanghai (69.5%). As for the top 5 cities in terms of patent applications, Beijing, Shenzhen and Shanghai are significantly better in both quantity and quality than Guangzhou and Hangzhou.

[Chart showing patent data for cities: Beijing, Shanghai, Shenzhen, Hangzhou, Guangzhou, Nanjing, Wuhan, Chengdu, Suzhou, Xi'an, Tianjin, Hefei, Chongqing, Changsha, Jinan, Xiamen, Zhengzhou, Qingdao, Guiyang, Fuzhou]

■ the number of patent applications ── the ratio of iuvention patent applications(right axis)

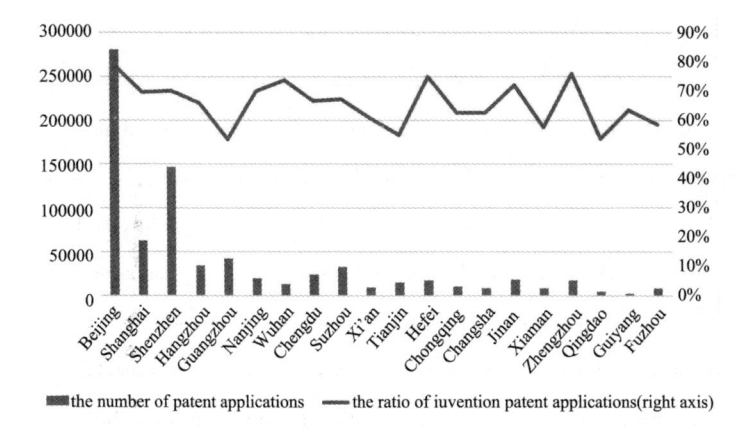

Graph 5 – 3: The Quantity and Quality of FinTech Patents in The FT20 Cities

Source: Calculated by SixLens and the Fintech Research Group of the Institute of Finance and Banking, Chinese Academy of Social Sciences.

5.2.2 The Distribution of FinTech Patents in the Industrial Chain

To further analyze the patents of FinTech enterprises, this report explores the distribution of these companies' patent applications in the industrial chain. In general, similar to the distribution of FinTech enterprises, the number of patents in the midstream of the industry chain is the largest, reaching 85.1%, followed by that in the upstream (12.9%), and the least is in the downstream, only 2.0%. It further highlights that China's FinTech enterprises focus more on the midstream of the industrial chain of technology integration and output.

The distribution of the patents of FinTech enterprises in cities is quite different in the industrial chain. As is shown in Graph 5 – 4, among the top 20 cities in the FinTech FIRE index, the patents of

FinTech enterprises in Jinan, Beijing and Guangzhou all account for more than 90% in the midstream of the industrial chain, while those in Xi'an, Qingdao and Tianjin all account for more than 30% in the upstream of the industrial chain. Chongqing (24.6%), Nanjing (24.5%), Chengdu (22.6%) and Hefei (20.5%) also accounted for more than 20% of patents in the upstream. In comparison, the proportion of patents of FinTech companies in these cities in the downstream of the industry chain is extremely low, even lower than 1%, except those in Beijing, Shenzhen, Wuhan and Shanghai. It further shows that the financial institutions in China are evidently insufficient in providing financial services with independent digital technologies.

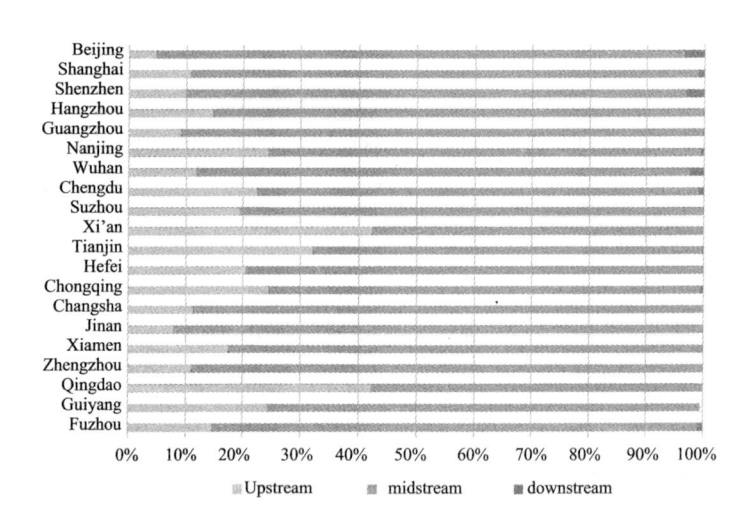

Graph 5-4: The Distribution of FinTech Enterprises of the FT20 Cities in the Industrial Chain

Source of data: Calculated by SixLens and the Fintech Research Group of the Institute of Finance and Banking, Chinese Academy of Social Sciences.

5.3 The Distribution of Digital Technology of FinTech

Digital technology is an important support for FinTech enterprises to improve their financial services. This report selected four key digital technologies from SixLens' global patent Investment and Financing Intelligence System to explore the distribution of technologies of FinTech enterprises in the upstream of industrial chain. These technologies selected are cloud computing, blockchain, big data and artificial intelligence.

5.3.1 The Regional Distribution of Digital Technology of FinTech Enterprises

Research and development of big data technology is the most engaged in FinTech enterprises. Graph 5 – 5 shows the engagement of FinTech enterprises in the four digital technologies. More than 8,500 companies are busy with the research and development of big data technology, which number is followed by that of cloud computing (1,090), and that of artificial intelligence is the smallest, only 323. The reason is that, as an important factor of production, big data is widely used while its threshold is relatively low.

The regional distribution of these technologies is quite different.

As is shown in Graph 16, among the top 20 cities in theFinTech FIRE index, Beijing, Shenzhen and Shanghai rank the top three with 1,363, 1,278 and 1,017 companies respectively, while Hangzhou (645), Guangzhou (503) and Tianjin (452) rank from the 4th to 6th. In terms of the four technologies, Hangzhou has the most FinTech companies engaged in cloud computing, Shenzhen has the most in blockchain, and Beijing has the most in big data and artificial intelligence.

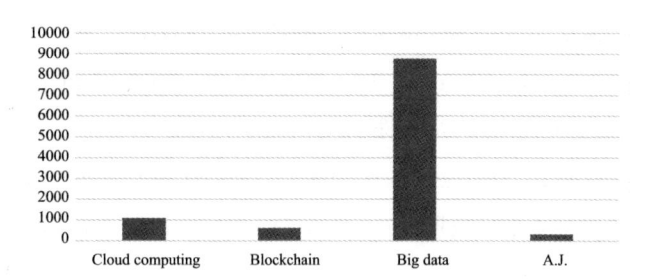

Graph 5-5: The engagement of FinTech enterprises in the four technologies

Source of data: Calculated by SixLens and the Fintech Research Group of the Institute of Finance and Banking, Chinese Academy of Social Sciences.

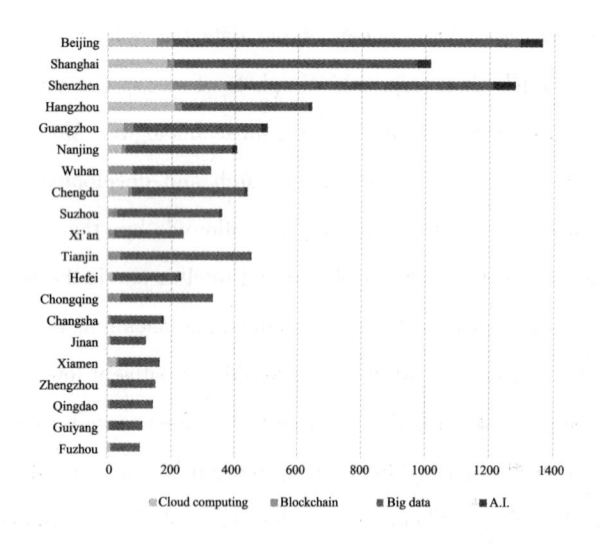

Graph 5-6: the regional distribution ofFinTech in the FT20 cities

Source of data: Calculated by SixLens and the Fintech Research Group of the Institute of Finance and Banking, Chinese Academy of Social Sciences.

5.3.2 The Regional Distribution of FinTech Digital Technology Patents

Patents of big data are of the most quantity, while patents of blockchain are of the highest quality. Graph 5 – 7 demonstrates that the number of patents of big data is the largest, over 100,000, far more than that of cloud computing, which is 3,318, let alone that of blockchain and artificial intelligence, more than 1,300 but fewer than 1,400. However, when it comes to the quality of patents, blockchain takes up most of the invention patents, accounting for 91.8% of the total, the next is that of cloud computing (85.0%), and the fewest goes to big data (42.8%).

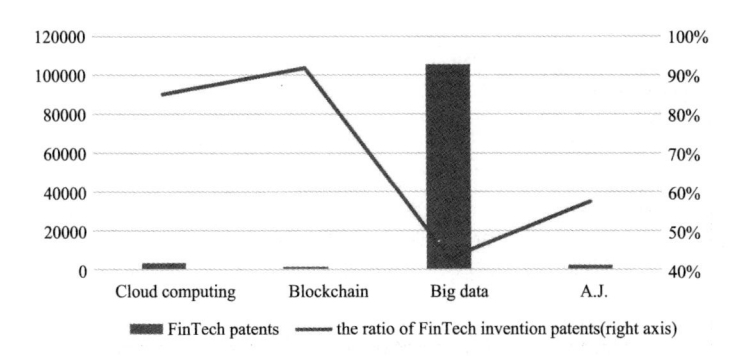

Graph 5 – 7: The distribution of FinTech technology patents

Source of data: Calculated by SixLens and the Fintech Research Group of the Institute of Finance and Banking, Chinese Academy of Social Sciences.

Beijing is clearly superior in the number of patents of cloud computing, blockchain and artificial intelligence. Graph 5 – 8 shows that for cloud computing, Beijing has the largest number of patents

(1,298), followed by Nanjing (650), Shenzhen (290) and Shanghai (222); for blockchain, Beijing still holds the most patents (521), followed by Shenzhen, Xi'an and Guangzhou with 181, 117 and 113, respectively; for big data, Shenzhen tops the list with 13,796 patents, followed by Beijing (10,756), Suzhou (6,313), Shanghai (6,113) and Hangzhou (4,875); for artificial intelligence, Beijing takes the 1st place with 705 patents, followed by Shanghai (437), Shenzhen (367), Guangzhou (190) and Chengdu (105).

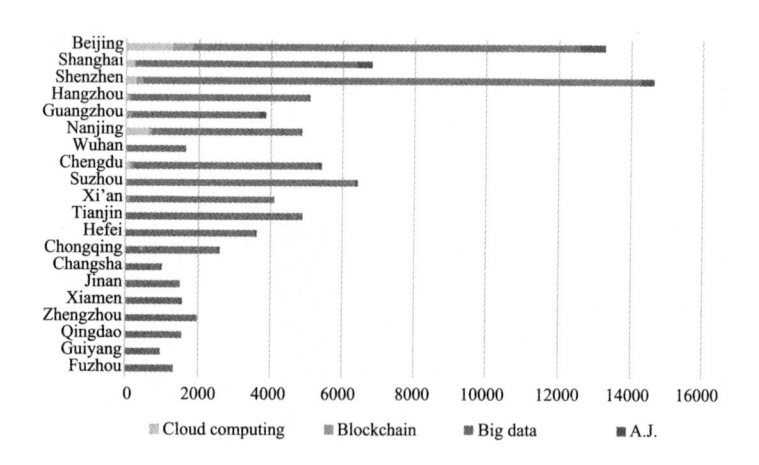

Graph 5 – 8: The distribution of FinTech technology patents in the FT20 cities

Source of data: Calculated by SixLens and the Fintech Research Group of the Institute of Finance and Banking, Chinese Academy of Social Sciences.

6
Conclusions and Prospects

6.1 Conclusions

6.1.1 China's FinTech FIRE Index

Based on the factors influencing FinTech, the research group designed an evaluation index system to explore the development of FinTech in different Chinese cities, with the four first-level indicators, which are Factors, Intelligence, Resources and Enterprises.

According to the list of China's FinTech FIRE Index, Beijing, Shanghai and Shenzhen take the first three places, and the rest of the top 10 cities are Hangzhou, Guangzhou, Nanjing, Wuhan, Chengdu, Suzhou and Xi'an. From the perspective of regional distribution, cities in east China outperform their counterparts in the west, central region and the northeast, while comparing with cities in north China, those in the south gain an upper hand.

As the ranking in terms of Factors is concerned, Beijing leads the chart, strong in economy and population; Hangzhou ranks the 2nd

for its strength in demographic dividend, especially in population growth; Guangzhou, Shanghai, Chongqing, Chengdu, Shenzhen, Changsha, Wuhan and Xi'an are the rest of the top 10 cities.

For the ranking from the perspective of Intelligence, Beijing tops the list, as it is superior in research in enterprises and universities; Shanghai and Nanjing take the 2nd and 3rd place, for their comparative advantages in research in universities and enterprises; Guangzhou, Shenzhen, Hangzhou, Wuhan, Chengdu, Xi'an and Tianjin are the rest of the top 10 cities.

For the ranking from the perspective of Resources, Shanghai takes the 1st place for its strength in policy, network and financial resources; Beijing and Shenzhen rank the 2nd and the 3rd for their noticeable performance in network and financial resources; Wuhan, Hangzhou, Nanjing, Chengdu, Guiyang, Xi'an and Guangzhou are the rest of the top 10 cities.

When it comes to the ranking from the perspective of Enterprises, Beijing outperforms the others for its absolute advantages in both the quantity and quality of enterprises; Shenzhen, Shanghai, Hangzhou, Guangzhou, Suzhou, Nanjing, Wuhan, Chengdu and Jinan are the rest of the top 10 cities.

6.1.2 The Regional Distribution of FinTech Enterprises and Their Positions in the Industrial Chain

This report investigates 50,436 FinTech enterprises in 59 cities, and collects patents of these enterprises for further analysis. The top 10 cities for both the number of FinTech companies and the number of patent applications are almost the same.

As for the quantity of FinTech enterprises, Beijing, Shanghai, Shenzhen, Guangzhou, Hangzhou, Chengdu, Nanjing, Suzhou, Wuhan and Tianjin are the top 10. FinTech enterprises in Beijing, Shanghai and Shenzhen, respectively account for 19.5%, 13.0% and 12.3% of the total in the country respectiely. The majority of them are in the middle of the industrial chain (74.2%), fewer of them are in the upstream (21.4%), and the fewest in the downstream (4.4%).

Patents are reflection of technological contribution in FinTech enterprises. In terms of patent applications, Beijing, Shenzhen, Shanghai, Guangzhou, Hangzhou, Suzhou, Chengdu, Nanjing, Jinan and Zhengzhou are the top 10. When it comes to the industrial chain, patent applications in the midstream are the most, taking up 85.1% of the total, followed by those in the upstream (12.9%) and those in the downstream (2.0%). As digital technologies are concerned, the number of companies engaged in the research and development of big data is the largest (8,500), followed by that of cloud computing (1,090), that of blockchain technology (611), and that of artificial intelligence (323). Patents of big data technology are of the largest quantity (105,481), followed by cloud computing (3,318), artificial intelligence (2,426), and blockchain (1,423). In terms of the quality of patents, blockchain holds the highest proportion of invention patents (91.8%), followed by cloud computing (85.0%), artificial intelligence (57.4%), and big data (42.8%).

6.2　Policy Recommendations

6.2.1　To Support the Development of FinTech with More Locally-Adapted Policies

Governmental support is crucial to the development of FinTech. The local government should play its part to make overall plans for the development of FinTech, releasing local FinTech development plans and other policies and measures to actually support the development of FinTech. With policy support, capital should be allocated more rationally, more investment should be encouraged in FinTech enterprises, especially to help the development of small and medium-sized FinTech enterprises, eliminating their difficulties in financing.

6.2.2　To Develop FinTech in Accordance with the Local Reality

The development of FinTech is imbalanced between regions. FinTech is well developed in Beijing, Shanghai and Shenzhen, where resources are plentiful and all relevant factors are in leading positions. For these cities, they should continue to maintain the virtuous circle of innovation-driven research and development to improve technologies to enable scenarios. For other cities, since resources are not that abundant, they should boost the development in accordance with their local realities, making up for their weaknesses while taking advantages of their strengths.

6.2.3 To Promote the Construction of Financial Infrastructure with the Release of Digital Currency by the Central Bank

In 2020, a pilot project for the digitalyuan is being carried out nationwide, and the digital currency will profoundly change the financial infrastructure. At present, the People's Bank of China has basically established the system of "two databases and three centers" for digital currency issuance, as well as the digital wallet at the client side. The four state-owned banks—Industrial and Commercial Bank of China, Agricultural Bank of China, Bank of China, and China Construction Bank, together with the three telecom operators—China Mobile, China Telecom and China Unicom, are participating in the pilot program conducted in Shenzhen, Suzhou, Xiong'an and Chengdu as well as in the upcoming Winter Olympics scenarios. Local governments should take this opportunity to step up the construction of key financial infrastructure and promote the application of emerging technologies, such as blockchain, big data, cloud computing and digital wallet, in digital currency.

6.2.4 To Advance the Coordinated Development of FinTech within City Clusters for Northern Cities

Northern cities should learn from the experience of southern cities. Taking the Beijing-Tianjin-Hebei city cluster as an example, they should strengthen regional cooperation, and promote the coordinated development of FinTech as a whole. According to the FinTech FIRE Index ranking, there is a big gap between the north and the south in terms of regional distribution. Among cities sorted in the first and second classes, Beijing is the only northern city, while cities from the south are relatively balanced in development, including three cities in the Yangtze River Delta city cluster and two cities in the Guangdong-Hong Kong-Macao Greater Bay Area. Cities in the northern region should gain the sense of "regional integration", to make more policy efforts to promote regional economic integration, strengthen the interaction and cooperation between cities in the region, and realize the coordinated development of FinTech within the region.

6.2.5 To Achieve All-round Development with the Development of FinTech for Central and Western Cities

Central and western cities should seize the opportunity of the integration of finance and technology, to make great efforts in the development ofFinTech and narrow the financial gap between the east and the west. The imbalance between the east and the west has been a while, which is reflected in various fields and industries. As is seen in the rankings from the perspective of regional distribution, there is an obvious east-west gap in the development of FinTech. Among the cities ranked in the first and second classes, six are located in the east, while only one is in the central part and one in the west. In recent years, with the wide application of emerging technologies such as big data, artificial intelligence and blockchain in the financial field, finance and technology have been integrated deeper and deeper. The central and western cities should follow the trend to strengthen theoretical research on FinTech, deepen cooperation among industries, universities and research institutes, accelerate the transformation of scientific research results to products and services, and realize an all-round development in FinTech. At the same time, it is necessary to grasp the historical opportunity of the "Belt and Road" Initiative, to use financial technology to provide better financial services for the countries in the "Belt and Road" areas, and to achieve the leap-forward economic development in the central and western regions.

6.2.6 To Boost the Development of RegTech

After the Fifth National Financial Work Conference, the central government issued a document to further clarify the regulatory powers of local governments over seven types of institutions and four types of scenarios. However, at present, the off-site supervision system established by local financial supervisors is tooextensive to meet the requirements of local financial supervision under the new situation. Therefore, in order to satisfy the demand of industry supervision, risk monitoring and early warning, coordinated supervision, and FinTech service management, RegTech should be strengthened in application to enhance the off-site supervision of the existing businesses and the sandbox regulation of innovative businesses. Together with on-site supervision, the vulnerable points should be overcome to improve the capacity and efficiency of local financial supervision.

6.3 Prospects

FinTech has become the core competitiveness of the financial industry. In order to further regulate the development of FinTech and let finance better serve the real economy, we should keep improving the research of FinTech, and figure out the direction of the development of FinTech in the future.

6.3.1 To Take the Development of FinTech as a National Strategy

At present, China has made good achievements in the development of FinTech, which makes China at the forefront of FinTech growth. In order to maintain this momentum, it is necessary to take the development of FinTech as a national strategy, making full use of FinTech as a driving force to upgrade the financial industry, facilitating China better participate in the international financial system, and raising China's voices in the international financial system.

6.3.2 To Accelerate the Establishment of a "Dual Circulation" Pattern with Greater FinTech Development

Under the influence of COVID-19 pandemic, in order to protect China's economic security and boost its economic development, the Fifth Plenary Session of the 19th CPC Central Committee put forward the major strategic deployment of accelerating the construction of a "dual circulation" development pattern in which domestic economic cycle lays a leading role while international economic cycle remains its extension and supplement. FinTech is the best way to promote financial development and the integration of production and financing, which can facilitate the establishment of "dual circulation" development. On the one hand, it can make breakthrough in the dollar system of the international financial system by innovating the payment and settlement system. On the other hand, it can also precisely access to macro-control policies to provide high-quality financial services for the supply-side structural reform and industrial structure optimization and upgrading.

6.3.3 To Establish a Multi-level FinTech Ecosystem with the Deep Integration of Finance and Technology

Nowadays, China's financial industry is mainly composed of traditional banking, securities, insurance, funds and other financial institutions. With the development of FinTech, a multi-level FinTech ecosystem is taking shape, which covers regulators, traditional financial institutions, FinTech companies, RegTech companies and technology companies. As the integration of finance and technology goes deeper, the ecosystem is growing larger, more diversified and more sophisticated. However, it should be noted that the construction of the multi-level FinTech ecosystem requires a balanced financial industry system, prevent systemic financial risks and protect the national financial security.

6.3.4 To Improve the Efficiency of Financial Supervision with the Rise of RegTech

The development of FinTech has not only boosted the development of the financial sector, but also raised risks for finance and technology. Regulators should employ human, material and financial resources, together with emerging technologies, such as artificial intelligence, big data, blockchain, and cloud computing, to constantly increase the application of RegTech in the development of FinTech, so as to improve the capacity and efficiency of supervision. At the same time, China should actively participate in international financial regulatory cooperation and guard against cross-border contagion of risks caused by FinTech.

6.3.5 To Ameliorate the Regulatory System of FinTech and Provide Policy Support for the Development of FinTech

FinTech and financial supervision promote each other and grow together. The emergence and development of FinTech promote the reform of financial supervision, while the effectiveness of financial supervision in turn determines the upper limit of FinTech growth. Therefore, we should establish a financial regulatory system that can meet the demand of the development of FinTech. At the macro level, we should set up a new concept of development, boost the construction of risk control mechanism, and establish a FinTech regulatory framework. At the micro level, we should implement the "three-line defense" risk control system to avoid major risks; and to improve regulation efficiency, we should provide more policy support for the development of FinTech to push the digital transformation of the financial sector, and we should promote the development of China's financial industry to surpass other countries and strengthen its international competitiveness.

Postscript

At present, the development of FinTech in China has come to a key period. During its transitioning from high-speed growth to high-quality development, risks and problems accumulated in the past have gradually come to light, in return to which, regulations on FinTech are tightened constantly. In this context, hot issues like how to measure the overall development of FinTech in China and its global status in an objective manner, how to estimate the development difference among the regions and figure out the regional and industrial chain distribution characteristics of FinTech companies, have become common concerns to local governments, regulatory authorities and the financial industry. Therefore, the FinTech Index research group is set up, based on the department of FinTech in the Institute of Finance and Banking (IFB), CASS, relying on the construction of the FinTech database.

The director-general of the research group is Prof. Hu Bin, who writes the preface in the book. The executive director of this project is Prof. Yin Zhentao, who is in charge of the research framework. The establishment of the Index and data sources are done by Ding Yi and Wang Yong. The first and sixth chapters are written by Zhang

Shufen. The second and third chapters are written by Zhang Yu. The fourth chapter is written by Ding Yi. The fifth chapter is written by Wang Yong. The translation of the book is done by Han Yang. The overall compilation and edit are done by Prof. Hu Bin, Prof. Yin Zhentao and Wang Yong.

When doing research and writing this book, the research group has received great supports from the People's Daily Digital Communication, the SixLens and Zhongke Qingbo. Many thanks should also be extended to those working in China Social Sciences Press and the Publishing Center for Chinese Social Sciences Think Tank Achievements, for their hard work and strong supports.

This book focuses on the construction of FinTech index. Due to the limitation of data and other factors, there may be deficiencies in the research. Suggestions and corrections are welcome.

HU Bin, Party Secretary and Deputy Director-General of the Institute of Finance and Banking (IFB), Chinese Academy of Social Sciences (CASS), is professor and supervisor for Ph. D. candidates. He also has positions as Deputy Director-General of the National Institution of Finance and Development, CASS. He has hosted more than 40 research projects, including major projects sponsored by the National Social Science Fund and CASS. He has published two books in English and one translation work, and over 100 papers on leading law and economics journals in China. He has been the editor-in-chief for the *Annual Report on China's Financial Supervision and Regulation* for 10 years. He was awarded with the "Youth Innovation Award" by Central State Organs Work Committee in 2010. Besides, professor Hu has gained a lot of outstanding awards from several organizations for his excellent policy research. He has been appointed the state's young and middle-aged expert with outstanding contribution of the National Talent Project and held Special Government Allowance of the State Council from 2014. Professor Hu has extensive experience and professional knowledge in the fields of financial regulation, FinTech, and inclusive finance, etc.

YIN Zhentao, is an associate professor and supervisor for postgraduates. He received his doctor's degree at the Institute of Economics, Chinese Academy of Social Science (CASS) in 2009. Now he works as the director of the Department of FinTech in the Institute of Finance and Banking (IFB), CASS. He also takes the position as secretary-general of the Research Center for Financial Law and Regulations under National Institution for Finance and

Development. He has published two academic monographs, one translation work and over fifty papers in core journals such as Economic Perspectives, Chinese Rural Economy, International Economic Review and Chinese Journal of Population Science. He has hosted and participated in several major projects sponsored by the National Social Science Fund and projects at the provincial or ministry level. Dr. Yin was honored "Young Chinese Economist" in 2014, and awarded the Third Prize of "The Ninth Chinese Academy of Social Sciences Excellent Scientific Research Achievements Award" in 2016. His major research areas include the financial supervision and regulation, financial risks and FinTech, etc.

WANG Yong, Ph. D. and post-doctor in economics, is an assistant researcher in theDepartment of FinTech in the Institute of Finance and Banking (IFB), CASS. He has published several papers in well-known journals such as Journal of Financial Research, Studies of International Finance, Journal of Finance and Economics, and China Soft Science. His main research fields include FinTech, Macro-finance and Economic Policy Evaluation, etc.